Critical Praise for Yisroel's first book "The Hidden Path"

"Through wisdom and wit, using an eclectic array of sources, Yisroel conveys many inspiring ideas about Judaism as well as gentle guidance on how to lead a more meaningful life.

—Former Senator and Vice-Presidential Candidate Joseph Lieberman

"A book that masterfully pulls together the most inspirational, understandable and accessible wisdom on some of the most important foundation concepts of Judaism. Throughout the book, Yisroel Juskowicz's love of G-d bursts forth on every page, lifting the reader into chapter after chapter, always wanting more."

—Lori Palatnik, author, international speaker, Founding Director of The Jewish Women's Renaissance Project

"Yisroel's book is full of great stories, insights and ideas designed to help its reader better appreciate Judaism and a connection to Hashem."

—Charlie Harary, Esq. world renowned speaker, radio show Host

"Yisroel Juskowitz is an artist and musician. He has succeeded in making music and art out of the fundamental principles of Yiddishkeit. "The Hidden Path" is an inspiring introduction to the beauty of being a Jew."

—Rabbi Moshe Weinberger

"Through heartfelt stories and meaningful parables, Yisroel empowers his readers to reach their unlimited potential. This inspiring book is written for anyone looking to deepen their relationship with G-d and themselves."

—Aleeza Ben Shalom, the Marriage Minded Mentor, author of Get Real, Get Married

"The saying goes, 'Words that are said from the heart go straight into the heart.' Reb Yisroel's soft spoken easy to digest style complement his inspirational message, making this new book a work that has the capacity to speak to everybody—no matter where they are on their personal journey at the present moment."

~ *Rabbi Eliyahu Yaakov, author of Jewish by Choice and The Case for Judaism*

"Yisroel Juskowitz weaves together beautiful words of Torah, heartwarming stories and accounts of his own personal journey to present this heartfelt work on essential Jewish topics. His sweetness and authenticity shines through on every page."

~ Rabbi Shlomo Buxbaum, Executive Director of Aish of Greater Washington

Also by Yisroel Juskowitz

Music:

The Narrow Bridge and *Fixing the World*
both critically acclaimed albums

Book:

The Hidden Path Yisroel's first book
available at kodeshpress.com

Art:

Fine art, calligraphy, and micrography Judaica

Audio:

Coming soon *The Hidden Path* and *For Every Season* audio series

All available at www.yisroeljuskowitz.com

For music and speaking engagements and Life
Coaching, visit www.yisroeljuskowitz.com

For Every Season

Illuminating Insights into the Jewish Holidays

"It is He who changes the times and the epochs; He removes kings and establishes kings; He gives wisdom to wise men and knowledge to men of understanding."

—Daniel 2:21

"The theme of every Jewish Holiday: They tried to kill us, we won, let's eat."

—old Jewish joke

Yisroel Juskowitz

KODESH PRESS

Published & Distributed by
Kodesh Press L.L.C.
sales@kodeshpress.com

This book is dedicated to my two beautiful children, Noach Daniel and Gavriel Dovid, for being my greatest little teachers, and lighting up my life in more ways that I could even imagine.

Chapter Dedications

Foreword: Why Care about the Holidays? Dedicated by Barry Cohen in honor of his lovely wife Yvonne.

Rosh Hashana: The Gift of Judgement. Dedicated by Chaim and Fayge Kasdan in honor of their parents.

Yom Kippur: Confronting Ourselves. Dedicated by my parents Rabbi and Mrs Juskowicz in loving memory of their parents Alter, Tzipporah, Rabbi Nachum, and Sora Leah Liebowitz.

Sukkot: The Tabernacle of Peace. Dedicated by Rick and Cindy Zeitelman in honor of of the Rabbis and Rebbetzins who have taught them Jewish values and wisdom.

Shemini Azeret/Simchat Torah: Torah and Water: Our Life Force. Dedicated by Daniel Ratner in honor of his wife Ilana and is children, Liam, Lila, Shani, Shaya, and Maya Noa.

Chanukah: Shattering Darkness with Light. Dedicated by Rick and Cindy Zitelman in honor of their children and grandchildren.

Tu B'shvat: A Celebration of Life. Dedicated by Steven Weinstock in honor of his parents Anna and Sam Weinstock.

Purim, the Story of Masks and Revelations. Dedicated by Christine and Aaron Inhen in honor of their son Theodore Atticus.

Passover: A New Journey as Old As Time. Dedicated by Steven Weinstock in honor of his beautiful family.

The Modern-Day Jewish Holidays: God's Role in the Present Day. Dedicated by Anna Cavalier in honor of her husband Dr. Yefim Ephraim Cavalier.

The Fiery Embers of Lag Baomer. Dedicated by Victor Seletsky in loving memory of Yaakov Ben Shlomo.

Shavuot: Receiving the Book of Love. Dedicated by Dr. Mayer Green in honor of his beautiful family.

Tisha B'av: Rising from the Ashes. Dedicated by Danielle Sorah Storch in honor of her husband Frankie's birthday.

Tu B'Av: The Jewish Holiday of Love. Dedicated by Ari Weintraub in honor of his beloved Zaidy Rabbi Nachum Liebowitz.

Table of Contents

Foreword

Why Care about the Holidays?

For everything there is a season, and a time for every matter under heaven:
a time to be born, and a time to die;
a time to plant, and a time to pluck up what is planted;
a time to kill, and a time to heal;
a time to break down, and a time to build up;
a time to weep, and a time to laugh;
a time to mourn, and a time to dance;
a time to cast away stones, and a time to gather stones together;
a time to embrace, and a time to refrain from embracing;
a time to seek, and a time to lose;
a time to keep, and a time to cast away;
a time to tear, and a time to sew;
a time to keep silence, and a time to speak;
a time to love, and a time to hate;
a time for war, and a time for peace.

-Ecclesiastes 3

OK, SO I ADMIT, WHEN it comes to this question of why care about the Holidays, I am a little bit biased. And that is, because, I *love* the Jewish Holidays. I have observed them my whole life, and they are

13

days that I usually look forward to throughout the year. This isn't even just for the "fun" holidays such as Chanukah and Purim, but even the more difficult ones, such as Tisha B'av and Yom Kippur. However, it wasn't *always* this way. In fact, growing up, I used to *dread* the holidays. This is because it took me away from my very valuable time, which mainly consisted of television and video games. In fact, I used to be either watching TV or playing video games right up till the very last minute before the holiday started, when either my mother or father came into the room and turned off the screen (this was pre-remote days when people actually had to go up to the screen to turn it off, if one can imagine such ancient times. I won't starting naming which shows and which video games I was into, since then I would *really* be dating myself.) And so I would grunt and groan and drag myself to the synagogue for services. But as time wore on, I outgrew my old habits and "grew up" into new ones. This was a bigger appreciation for the more meaningful things in life, but also a different understanding into what these things were. And I actually came to love the holidays. However, the reasons *why* I have come to love them may help illuminate the significance to these unique days and provide warmth and comfort for you as well. In a moment, I will explain.

But before I begin to explain, I wanted to share with you a story that I heard from *Rabbi David Aaron*, the founder and dean of Isralight Institute in Israel. He talked about a time he went to meet a great well-known Kabbalist. He was very excited to meet this Kabbalist known for his priceless pearls of wisdom. When he went to meet the great Kabbalist, the Kabbalist offered him an apple. Rabbi Aaron thought, this is easy, an apple represents wisdom. When he reached out to take the apple from him, the Kabbalist pulled the apple back. The Kabbalist offered it to him a second time. Again, Rabbi Aaron tried to take it from him and again the Kabbalist pulled back. Finally, on the third time, Rabbi Aaron got the message. On the third time, when the Kabbalist offered him the apple, instead of reaching to *take* the apple, he put out his hand palm up to *receive* the apple. This time, the Kabbalist placed the apple into his hand. The message of this simple story is very profound and powerful. To be able to learn, one must first make oneself into a vessel that is ready to *receive* wisdom. Even the word Kabbalah comes from the word *Kabel* which means "to receive." This is the message I wanted to convey when starting this book and really for getting the most out of Judaism in general. In order to get the most out of the wisdom that the Torah has to offer, one must make oneself into a vessel that is ready to receive. One must open his or her heart and then the Divine Wisdom will flow inside.

Our journey begins with a paradigm shift in how we are to view the Holidays themselves. We are taught by our Sages that God looked into the Torah and then created the world. It is specifically in *this* order, and not the other way around. How are we to understand this? We know many of the most significant events contained in the Torah did not occur till much later, long after creation of the world. What does it mean that the Torah actually preceded creation? The answer becomes apparent when we begin to look at the purpose of creation. We are taught that the purpose of the world was to have the opportunity to bring ourselves closer to God, and as such these forces were set in motion even before the creation of the world. This was the script, or "blueprint" so to speak, and from this blueprint, Creation sprang. The world was designed as a giant arena with tribulations that can distance us from Him as well as opportunities to bring ourselves closer to Him. When an architect designs a skyscraper, he or she generally knows what purposes the building will serve and thus designs the building accordingly. If the Torah was "written" so to speak, even before the world as we know it existed, that means the Holidays, (which are written about in the Torah) existed even *before* the events that they commemorate occurred! *This means that the Holidays are more than just commemorations, they are actual energies that are inherent in those days.* When we celebrate a Holiday we are doing much more than just commemorating a past event, we are *tapping* into the energy that is inherent on that day. This energy existed even before the event of the holiday.

We see this idea most succinctly in the story of Abraham. Abraham was the first Jew who discovered God at a young age, passed a series of ten difficult tests to show his faith in God, and became the father of a new people. As such, we know, according to the Talmud, he was granted prophecy, and was blessed with the Divine Spirit to know about events that would occur in the future. One of these tests was when three angels appeared to him in the guise of men, and Abraham, in the heat of the day, having just endured circumcision, still went out to perform the *Mitzvah* of greeting guests. The verse says he asked his wife Sarah to prepare "cakes" for these guests. The *Midrash* explains that these "cakes" were actually *Matzah* since this incident occurred during the days when the holiday of Passover would later occur. Abraham knew through the Divine Spirit that these days would one day be Passover, the days when the Jewish People would miraculously be saved from slavery in Egypt. The question of course, is why was Abraham celebrating these days? The events didn't occur till centuries later? What possibly could be the significance of commemorating something which never even happened yet? Given what we explained above, the answer is quite simple. The Holidays are much more than just commemoration. Even before the events of the Holiday took place, there was already a certain spiritual energy that existed on those days, and the events that occurred on those days was merely an outgrowth of that energy. And by celebrating the Holiday, *even before the events of the Holiday occurred,* a person is tapping into that incredible spiritual energy. It reminds me of when the crew from the Starship Enterprise used to get beamed up to a distant planet. (I know I am dating myself a lot here and anyone under the age of 35 probably has no idea what I am talking about.) They used to go to this special room and stand over a teleportation area and get beamed up to go to a distant planet. This is kind of how I view the Holidays, although it would be pretty sacrilegious to draw a full comparison to Judaism from a science fiction show. When a Holiday comes it is as if we are standing over the teleportation area and getting transported to the time and place when the events occurred. The beautiful Sephardic custom on Passover Seder night of walking around the table carrying a sack of food as if they were leaving Egypt hints to this idea. It isn't just *commemorating*, it is *reliving*. It is experiencing the events in real time, on that day. But it is more than even that, we aren't only being transported to the original day of the Holiday, we are being transported to the *energy* contained in the day, an energy which existed long before the events of the Holiday even occurred.

This is of course, a radical new approach to the Jewish Holidays, as sadly enough, the vast majority of Jews merely think of the

Holidays as commemoration and nothing more. The reality is that the commemoration aspect is just the beginning of understanding what the Holidays are. They are that, but also so much more.

There is another reason why the Holidays are so meaningful to me, and in turn, I believe can be so much more meaningful to you, dear Reader. Let me share with you a beautiful teaching about Purim from the *Baal Shem Tov*, the founder of the Chassidic movement. Regarding reading the *Megillah,* the Talmud teaches that if one were to read the story backwards, one would not fulfill his or her obligation. What does this mean? No one would read the Megillah backwards! *The Baal Shem Tov* explains this law on a deeper level. If one were to read the Megillah backwards, meaning *if one were to read it as if it is just an event in the past that is irrelevant to us today, one has not fulfilled his or her obligation.* The story of Esther is very much relevant to us today. As true as this is about Purim, it is just as true about *all* the Jewish Holidays.

What makes the Holidays so awesome is that they really capture *us*; the enormous vicissitudes of life that we experience throughout our lives. Our lives have moments of triumph and joy, but also moment of sadness and loss. There are times in our lives when we experience trepidation as we are forced to confront our own shortcomings. And there are times when we can revel in the comforts and warmth of being with the people who mean the most to us. This is what the Holidays are all about; experiencing each year the entire gamut of human emotion, but through the Jewish experience. On Rosh Hashanah, we do the introspection that many of us do in our personal lives. On Passover we surround ourselves by our family and bask in the glow of our beautiful traditions. On Chanukah, we celebrate the miracle of the survival of our Faith over Hellenism. And on Tisha B'av, we experience the pain of our collective loss. On Shavuot, we combine our intellect and heart to connect to God through the study of His Torah and rediscovering the revelation at Sinai. The Holidays are more than the story of our collective People, they are the story of who we all are, all experienced in a yearly cycle. This is living Judaism, it is why our Holidays are so relevant to us today. They are a microcosm of our life experiences, set into a Jewish framework. We are all emotional beings, and as such we need to see Judaism in that way. Seeing the Holidays in this context is one of the ways to make it more meaningful. Therefore, I began the book with the well-known quote from Ecclesiastes since it captures the themes of our life cycle, and many of the themes of the Holidays as well. It is also why I decided that in each of these chapters I would write about that particular Holiday on the Holiday itself. Some Holidays have restrictions against writing during them, so for those Holidays I wrote about them right after the Holiday. This is because I felt it was the best way to capture the mood and experience of the Holiday on the Holiday itself.

In Kabbalistic literature, God is compared to the sun and the Jewish People are compared to the moon. Indeed, the Jewish cycle always centers after the moon. We follow the lunar calendar, and we bless the new moon each month. How are we to understand that God is compared to the sun, and we are compared to the moon? One way could be that we are meant to reflect God's light to the world, much in the way that the moon reflects the light of the sun to the world. However, I believe there is another analogy for how the sun represents God, and the moon the Jewish People. God is constant, He is ever Present, never changing, much like the sun. However, the Jewish People are ever changing, much like the moon, which waxes and wanes. We too, expand and diminish, throughout the year, as the yearly cycle and Jewish Holidays represent. We are "fullest," so to speak, during the joyful holidays, and "diminished," so to speak, during the Holidays that are tragic. We, as a People are never stagnated; we are always either growing in life, or receding. It is interesting to note that we say the blessing for the new month just as the sliver of moon begins to expand and can only say it when the moon is still expanding. Perhaps it is to help remind us of our role, to be constantly growing in our spirituality. It is no coincidence that the very first commandment of the Torah is to bless the New Moon, for much is taught through this commandment about true spiritual living.

The seasons that the Holidays occur in are also very much related to the Holidays themselves. It is no coincidence that Hanukah and Purim, which celebrate miracles that were more hidden occur during the wintertime, in the bitter cold when the days are shortened, and the nights are long. And it is no coincidence that Passover is in the spring, for the symbolism of redemption is when the flowers begin blooming and the earth once again is renewed. Shavuot continues at the height of the spring, when the earth is fully renewed, for the Torah is called the Tree of Life. It is only in the spring that we can be ready to accept the Torah. For the same way the springtime gives life and sustenance to the earth for the year, so too the Torah gives sustenance to our souls each year.

There is a parable I shared in my first book *The Hidden Path* that is worth repeating now, when discussing the holidays. For those who haven't read my first book (ahem), now of course, would be a good time to pick up a copy. The parable came from *Nachmanides* (Ramban), one of the greatest Jewish scholars from the Middle Ages. He writes that all of life is like we are walking through a thunderstorm, in a forest at night. All too often we stumble, feeling lost, without direction. However, every now and then, there is a flash of lightning, where suddenly the world around us is illuminated, and we can see where we are going. We then must use the memory of what we saw in that flash of lightning to continue to guide us through that forest.

The Holidays are those flashes of lightning. They are the anchors which give our lives purpose. They are the times when we can step back from the rat race of life and remember what matters most. When we go to sleep each night, the last thing many of us do is plug in our cellphones to recharge it for the next day. The Holidays arewhat recharge our souls. They are what invigorate us to continue to go through the daily grind, for they are what make our lives worth living.

Moreover, there is a beautiful verse in the Book of Psalms which illustrates this idea even further. In the verse, King David writes "One thing I ask from God, one thing which I beseech from Him. To *dwell* in His House all the days of my life, to behold the grace of the Lord, and to *visit* in His Sanctuary." It is interesting that right here in the same verse it first says to *dwell*, which connotes permanence, but then uses the word *visit*, which connotes transience! How are we to understand this? I heard a beautiful answer once from a Rabbi in Memphis. When we dwell somewhere permanently, we begin to feel a sense of complacency. The excitement of being in that place soon loses its effect, and we begin to have a sense of dullness. However, a visitor will have that higher level of excitement since his location appears new and fresh to him or her. This is how it is with our connection to God. We are always in His Presence, and therefore very often our connection to Him begins to feel stagnant and rote. However, there are a few days every year when we can once again feel like we are visitors in the Presence of God. These days are the Holidays. During these days we can one again feel a sense of newness, a sense of excitement to be in His Presence, for we are more closely in His Presence during these days.

One brief word of thanks to the many people in my life who continuously help encourage me to better myself, as well as the people who helped transform this book from a dream into a reality. Please forgive me in advance if I leave anyone out. First and foremost, to my wonderful parents and siblings, whose love and encouragement has continued to help me grow daily. My parents especially have taught not only to *know* the Torah, but to *love* it as well. To my two beautiful children, Noach Daniel and Gavriel David, my greatest teachers, whose sweet innocence and love have deepened my relationship to God every day. To the amazing Kelly Paul for all her selflessness and care. To the many friends and family who contributed financially to make this project finally happen. To my *Rebbi, Rabbi Moshe Weinberger*, who continues to impact me, through his Torah classes, even hundreds of miles away. And finally, to the One Above, for giving me a few gifts, and who, despite my flaws, has given me the lifelong opportunity to get close to Him.

One brief word about the cover of the book. I did this one in pastel. It shows the great Jewish Clock so to speak, of the year with the background divided into the four seasons and the twelve "hours" on the clock represented by each of the holidays, as they fall into their corresponding seasons in the background. I chose to use this painting of mine since I believe it reflects the cyclical vibe of our special Jewish calendar. However, a Jew, a *real* Jew, does not travel through the yearly cycle in a *circular* fashion. A real Jew, a *soulful* Jew experiences each year in a *spiral* fashion. We are not at the same point we were last year on a given holiday; rather we have traveled upwards, even though we may be at the same time of the year. A Jew does not remain stagnant, as long as we are here, as long as we breathe, we must grow, always grow. We are not *crawling* through life, we are *dancing* through life. Life is always about growth. This is real spiritual living.

It is for these reasons, and many more that you will see in these pages, that the Holidays are so meaningful for me, and I believe can be meaningful to you as well. I invited you my dear Reader, to come along with me for my first journey through my first book *The Hidden Path*. Although this book is self-contained, in a very real way, it is a continuation of my first book. For the first book contained many different facets to Judaism and life, and ways to grow from each of them. So too, this book, which is on the Holidays, is a pathway toward self-growth, for that is the sole purpose for why the Holidays were given to us. I encourage everyone to read the chapter on each Holiday thirty days before the beginning of the Holiday, as according to Jewish custom, preparation for each holiday should begin then. I myself wrote each chapter in the days leading up to each Holiday, and, when permissible, wrote on the Holiday itself. Each Holiday is an opportunity to discover parts of ourselves and can be used as a springboard to help us reach our potential. Once again, I invite you to come along with me for the ride. Welcome back, my dear friends. It has been too long. The Holidays will never feel the same again...

With Love,

Yisroel

Silver Spring, Maryland

Rosh Hashanah: The Gift of Judgment

"Today is the Birthday of the world. Today all creatures of the world stand in judgment-whether as children or as servants. If as children, please be merciful with us as a father for children. If as servants, our eyes look toward You, until You be gracious toward us and release our verdict pure as light, oh Awesome and Holy One."

—Rosh Hashanah Prayer

W E ALL HATE IT WHEN someone judges us. Most of us right away turn on the defense mechanisms when we are being judged. We often say "Who are you to judge me? You are not in my shoes!" Or sometimes we say something even more indignant "Oh and *you* are any better? Are *you* a perfect person?" And when we do have to stand in judgment in front of someone (nearly everyone has been to traffic court at some point in their lives), we often feel uncomfortable, like every move we make is carefully being placed under the microscope. We start trying to think of ways to improve the situation. And often, when we know we are completely wrong, the embarrassment and shame that it entails can be unbearable. People can be racked with guilt, sometimes to the point of debilitation.

The last thing we usually associate with judgment is love. Judgment is something we usually associate with harshness, which sometimes may feel the opposite of love. Judaism teaches that really the opposite is true. Judgment is the epitome of love. Please allow me to explain.

I once heard a story about a teenage Jewish boy who tried to take his own life. Thankfully, he was stopped before he was able to complete what he was trying to do. Shortly after this, he was assigned to meet with a rabbi and discuss why he had tried to commit suicide. The answer he gave was quite startling. He revealed to the rabbi that his parents were divorced, after his mother ran off with some guy, and he had not spoken to his mother in years. He had no other siblings, so the only family he had in his life was his dad. His dad was very wealthy but had very little time for him. Soon his father began dating someone, and the relationship seemed to be going well. The only caveat was that she didn't want the "hassle" of having a teenage boy in her life, so soon the boy became a burden to his father as well. One day his father went over to him and said he would buy his son his own apartment and a sports car, and mail him a check for $5,000 each month, but he is to never come back to his father's home again. It was shortly after this new living arrangement that the teenage boy tried to commit suicide.

On a surface level, many teenagers would say they would *dream* for this! Having their own apartment without having to pay for it? A new sports car? $5,000 every month! And best of all, no parents "breathing down their neck" telling them what they can and cannot do! Yet, this "dream" lifestyle for a teenager drove him to attempt suicide. Why? Because underneath the surface, everyone knows that love is about connecting, it is about building a relationship. And most importantly, it is about *caring*. It is about caring about every action of our loved one. For the opposite of Love is not Hate. It is *indifference.* It is not knowing and not caring to know. This drove this young boy to attempt suicide, when he felt the only one left from his family had stopped caring.

This is the way to approach judgment on Rosh Hashanah. A God who loves us is a God who cares about us. And caring means being concerned for our well-being. Concerned about our actions. For ultimately, it is He, and only He who truly knows what is best for us. Many of us believe that we know what is best for us, but how much do we really know? Science has yet to uncover everything that there is to understand about a single cell, can we possibly say we understand everything? The only one who can really know everything about us, is the One who created us. It is that simple. A child wishes he or she could eat candy and ice cream all day. It is only the parent who understands the consequences of this who can tell the child it isn't good for him or her, and fruits and vegetables are important for one's diet. At the time the child may be upset at the parent but will one day understand that the parent had only the best interests for the child.

And so, we approach Rosh Hashanah with a paradoxical set of emotions. On the one hand, it is referred to as a Day of Awe, and even more harshly as a Day of Judgement, for we know that we are standing in front of the Almighty with our shortcomings fully exposed. But at the same time, it is a day of tremendous happiness as well, for it is a day that we truly can feel God's deep love for us, and to once again strengthen our relationship with Him.

This may very well explain two seemingly contradictory verses. In one verse it is written "We are to serve God with great joy" but in another verse it writes "We are to serve God with trepidation." How are we to reconcile this? Indeed, this is what Rosh Hashanah is all about. It is a day of joy and trepidation all at once. The day is called *Yom Hadin* or "Judgement Day" yet we are also obligated to celebrate it as a *Chag* (Festival) with eating and drinking at elaborate meals. This is how the Jew approaches this holy day, this is what makes this Jewish Holiday special and what makes our relationship with God so special, that we can approach Him with these two states of being at once.

With this insight we can understand some of the laws concerning the primary ritual of Rosh Hashanah itself, namely the blowing of the Shofar. The Shofar according to Jewish Law must be bent which indicates humility, yet it emits a powerful awe-inspiring cry. In fact, the Great Chassidic master *Rabbi Zadok Hakohen of Lublin* explains that that this is the primary reason for the way in which we blow Shofar! The custom is that each time we blow Shofar, we surround a broken sound (*Shevarim* or *Teruauh*) with one long straight sound (*Tikeah*) both before and after it. The broken sounds are meant to sound like wailing, thus symbolizing our own brokenness and trepidation. However, the long straight sound that surrounds the broken sounds is the joy we feel on this great day, the one long continuous blast.

This also helps to explain the seemingly wrong order of Rosh Hashanah and Yom Kippur. Yom Kippur, as we know, is the Day of Atonement for our sins and Rosh Hashanah is the Day of Judgement. Shouldn't the order be that we *first* have Yom Kippur, and only *afterward* Rosh Hashanah? Shouldn't we ask God for forgiveness first before we are judged? Shouldn't we show our remorse and our desire to better ourselves through the atonement process *before* we are judged? The answer is that Rosh Hashanah is more than just simply a day of Judgement, it is God looking at the world and seeing the Big Picture. He is remembering our relationship to Him. He wants to renew our relationship to Him and tell us He cares about us. Once we understand and feel this deeply rooted love, only then can we begin to share our shortcomings and then our desire to fix them.

Incidentally this is the same order we say in our daily prayers. In the *Amida*, the pinnacle of our daily prayers, we first ask God "*Hashiveynu Avinu Letoratecha,*" that is, "Please God, our Father, allow us to return to Your Torah" and then we say "*Slach Lanu Avinu Ki Chatanu*" which means "Please Our Father accept our forgiveness for we have sinned." We first *state our desired goals,* that is to come close to God, and only then do we discuss our roadblocks that prevent us from getting there. It is imperative that we know where we want to go first, and only then can we work to overcome the shortcomings that prevent us from getting there.

I learned this path and have used it successfully on many of my clients when working as a Life Coach. The first step toward true growth is stating the desired outcomes, and not only stating them but *feeling* them. I would do this through creating a Vision Statement for each client. Only then do we discuss the baby steps and hurdles needed to reach that ultimate vision. Rosh Hashanah is the Vision statement, Yom Kippur is the stated goals with discussing the obstacles that need to be removed to reach our goals.

Coronation of the King

This idea can help to explain one of the mysteries surrounding the Rosh Hashanah liturgy. On Rosh Hashanah we would expect the liturgy to be written in the form of deep introspection; that is of discussing our positive deeds as well as our wrongdoings. However, throughout the entire liturgy we barely discuss this at all. In fact, the words *Yom Hadin*, or Judgement Day is only mentioned several times. There are three main themes of the day, one of them is the theme of *Malchiot*, or Kingship. When discussing Kingship, we are discussing coronating God as our King. One of the deeper reasons, the mystics explain why we blow Shofar is because in Biblical times part of the coronation ceremony of a King was done with either trumpet or Shofar blasts. Why is it so important to discuss coronation of the King on our Day of Judgement? And furthermore, does God really need us to coronate Him? God as we know is not corporeal, and so there is nothing that we can give Him. So why bother with this charade of coronation?

Given what we explained above, we can understand what we hope to accomplish by the coronation of God as our King. Throughout the year and our many accomplishments, we can get arrogant, and start to believe that the world revolves around us. We can tend to believe that we are at the top of the world, and can start to develop a sense of selfishness, or at least of instant gratification. Rosh Hashanah represents a paradigm shift in how we view ourselves and the world. By coronating God as our King, we bring God into the center of our lives. Through this we come to accept our own fallibility and frailties and develop a renewed sense of purpose. Moreover, we come to look beyond ourselves and strive to reach our greater selves. Through this we get a glimpse of the Infinite.

It is for this reason why so much of the Rosh Hashanah liturgy focuses on *Malchut*, the Hebrew word for kingship. For on Rosh Hashanah we so to speak coronate God as our King, that is we accept His total sovereignty over the world. For through accepting His Reign we reach an understanding of what is important in life and accepting this reality into our lives. That is, we realign our vision with His Vision, and at last our visions become one. We recognize how to really lead a truly meaningful and content life. Seeing this is the ultimate Vision Statement.

The Call of the Shofar

The focal point of the Rosh Hashanah prayer services is undoubtedly the blowing of the Shofar. This is a powerful ritual so embedded in the

Jewish psyche that has been practiced universally, but many do not delve deeper into the spiritual underpinnings of the Shofar and the Shofar blasts. Let us take a few moments now to examine some of the rich symbolism and energies behind this great ritual.

The Lubavitcher Rebbe points out something remarkable about the Shofar, which gives us insight into not only the Holiday itself, but in general, our relationship with God. He points out that the Shofar is blown from the small and narrow side, but the sound emits from the larger, wider side. This, he explains brilliantly, is the secret to Shofar blowing, and how we approach God on Rosh Hashanah. We approach him with humility, recognizing our frailties, and our pettiness. It is from this small hole that the sound is first produced. But from here the sound gets louder as it expands to the wider side. As we approach God in this proper way, we can grasp at least slightly, His Divine Majesty, which in turn, elevates our own Divine Spark. It is therefore no coincidence that we begin the Shofar ritual with the following verse from Psalms: "From *the depths*, I called out to God, He answered Me from *His Heights*." That is, the very act of calling out to God from a low place helps us to then receive Him from a high place. For through our own smallness, we achieve greatness.

One of the most beautiful ideas I have ever learned on the blowing of the Shofar comes from the great *Rabbi Yitzchak Hutner,* in his monumental work *Pachad Yitzchak* (The Awe of Yitzchak). In it, he writes about one of the deeper more mystical ideas behind the Shofar. The Talmud writes that Rosh Hashanah does not really celebrate the creation of the world, but rather the creation of Man, the pinnacle of creation, and the first Rosh Hashanah was the day of the creation of Adam, the first human with a unique soul. The Torah writes that God breathed into Adam a *Nishmat Chaim*, loosely translated as a breath of life, but the word *Nishma* comes from the word *Neshama*, or soul. This is the great idea that God has so to speak breathed a part of Himself into each of us, and this Godly part is our soul. Moreover, it is the force which brings life into us.

What does this have to do with Shofar? The Shofar, as we know, is a horn from a dead animal, and yet when we blow into it, we make a sound and breathe life into it, as well as breathing life into ourselves. Thus, in a very real way the Shofar helps to awaken within us the Godly part of ourselves, to remind us of our soul which brings life to our bodies. Without it, our bodies are as good as dead, but with it, we are awakened to a higher place and a more inspired level of existence.

Moreover, for a Shofar to produce a sound, it must be completely hollow. If there is even any obstruction, the Shofar will not work. Once again, there is a deeper symbolism at play here. For one to grow, one must make oneself empty; that is to remove arrogance from one's heart. One must make oneself into a vessel that is ready to receive inspiration. It is for this reason that the Shofar must be bent, for being bent symbolizes humility. It is only through humility that one can be ready to receive what the sound of the Shofar truly means.

But there is something even more beautiful about the symbolism of the Shofar. The Talmud teaches us that the horn that we use for the Shofar must come from a ram. Why specifically the ram? The Talmud explains it has its origins from the *Akeda* story, as according to the commentators, the *Akeda* story took place on Rosh Hashanah. For those unfamiliar, the *Akeda* is one of the most powerful stories in the entire Bible. It is when Abraham was tested by God, the last of a series of ten trials, when he was asked by God to sacrifice his beloved son Isaac. He showed his willingness to comply with God's wishes but at the very last moment just as he raised the knife to slaughter his son, an angel came and stopped him. It was then that he was informed that this was all a test and that he had proved himself worthy to become the father of the Chosen People. Perhaps the most powerful line in the story is when the angel came and stopped him and called out "Abraham, Abraham" and Abraham answered "*Hineni*." This means "Here I am." It is an incredible affirmation for him, it was a moment when he realized he had found his greatest inner strength, it was the moment when he reached his potential. It was then that Judaism was born. At the end of the story, Abraham at that moment saw a ram caught in the thicket and he used this ram in the place of Isaac. It is this ram that is symbolized with the Shofar. This story of the *Akeda* is so central to Rosh Hashanah that it is read in its entirety from the Torah each year on the Holiday itself.

I believe that the ram of this story symbolizes what Rosh Hashanah means, and the message God is conveying to us. Rosh Hashanah is

29

more than a New Year, it is even more than a day of Judgement. It is a day of deep introspection, *it is a day to remember and discover the innate potential that is in each one of us.* What better way to do this than through this story, the story when Abraham discovered his own potential, when he was able to reach above and beyond himself to accept and obey God's will? What better way to discover our own potential than to remind us of how Abraham was able to fulfill his own potential in that crucial moment, and become the father of our People? And so the sound of the Shofar is literally and figuratively a wake-up call to ourselves to discover our own potential, just as Abraham did over 3,500 years ago. An inspiring message for Rosh Hashanah indeed.

The Power of Remembrance

We have discussed the themes Kingship (Malchut) and Shofar, but there is a third theme of Rosh Hashanah, which we have not explored yet, and that is the theme of *Zichronot*, or Remembrance. This is just as central in the prayers as the other two themes, and at times is even elevated to a higher state than the other themes. In fact, in the Kiddush as well as many of the most prominent prayers we call the Holiday *Yom Hazikaron*, or the Day of Remembrance. Why is remembrance so crucial to this Holiday? And what are we trying to remember?

We can answer the second question by looking at the Rosh Hashanah liturgy when the verses discussing remembrance are discussed. It seems as if the two main themes of the *Zichronot* are remembering Noah's Flood and remembering the Binding of Isaac, as we mentioned above. Why specifically these two themes?

One possible answer occurred to me when I was giving advice to one of my life coaching clients. This client was going through a very difficult time in her marriage and felt she was at a crossroads for whether or not she should continue her marriage. "We have been married for eleven years now. Our love has died, and it never seems to come back. I don't seem to have any feelings for him anymore, and he doesn't seem to have for me either anymore. We just go about our days in the same monotonous mind-numbing way," she moaned.

I sat and thought long and hard about their predicament. Suddenly an idea occurred to me. "Hey, you still have your wedding video, I assume? You know, the one collecting dust in your attic somewhere? How about the two of you watch it together? But don't just watch it, try to relive the experience as you are watching it, try to imagine as if you are there again right at that moment. Try to delve into the feelings and emotions you were experiencing during those powerful first moments in your marriage. And then report back to me after you try this exercise."

She reported back to me a few days later. Sure enough, it helped to rekindle the old feelings they once had for each other. I realized then what is so powerful about memory; *by remembering what once was,* we can get to a greater appreciation and understanding of things in the present state that we are in. The reason people are always taking photos and videos of their loved ones is so that later they can re-experience those moments and therefore cherish their loved ones even more.

Now we can go back to explain *Zichronot* and why specifically the story of Noah's flood as well as the story of the Binding of Isaac were chosen. Let us examine these two stories one at a time.

First let us examine the story of Noah. On the one hand, the story of Noah's flood was somewhat of a tragic watershed in the history of mankind, but on the other hand it was a powerful testament to Man's ability to remain steadfast in their own ethical convictions. On the one hand the story of the Flood was about the failings of Mankind; their inability to rise above temptations, for "the earth was filled with corruption" as the Torah writes. However, in the very same story we see the hope for Mankind, for Noah did not allow himself to be swayed by the corruption around him "A righteous man, perfect in his generation" as the Torah writes. Here in this story Mankind was given a second chance, a chance once again to find meaning and to search for God, and to choose to rise above the den of iniquities that often surround us. Furthermore, Mankind was given a sign at the end of the story; the sign of the rainbow, which was a promise that God would never again destroy His world. Thus, the story of Noah is a story of hope, and an affirmation to our purpose here in this world. From the story of Noah came the Seven Noahide Laws given to all of Mankind, seven universal laws of ethical behavior.

Now let us examine the second story, namely the story of the binding of Isaac. As mentioned before, this was the final test given to Abraham; where he displayed his ability to obey God's word, no matter how difficult God's request was. This was more than just the moment when Abraham reached his full potential. For it was after this trial that God informed Abraham that he will be the father of a people who will be "as numerous as the stars in the sky and the sand by the sea." It was there that God made the covenant with Abraham, it was there that the Jewish People were born.

So, let's return once again to our question; why specifically these two stories? The answer is extraordinary and inspiring; for within these two stories God now "remembers" both His reason for Humanity as well as His reason for His Chosen People. All of humanity can get close to God through the basic ethics which began through Noah, and the Jewish People were given a more specific mission, and it began with Abraham. It is through these two stories that God "remembers" so to speak, what once was. But it is not only for *God's* sake, so to speak, it is also for *our* sake, for when we recall these stories we re-experience them and reiterate to ourselves our own Divine Purpose.

A Rosh Hashanah Story

My favorite Rosh Hashanah story is the one told by *Rebbetzin Esther Jungreis*, about the Shofar of Bergen Belsen. Rebbetzin Jungreis, a Holocaust Survivor herself, witnessed this story firsthand. In the hellhole that was Bergen Belsen, a group of Jews managed to get to the stockpile which contained the Jewish holy items, by using cigarettes to bribe guards, and procured the sacred Shofar just in time for Rosh Hashanah. Incredibly, Jewish inmates of all walks of life and ages pressed into the bunker where the Shofar was blown. The first signs of life could be seen on the skeletal faces of those present as they listened to the ancient call of our tradition. In the camp next door, the Polish Jews also leaned forward to hear the millennial old cry. Soon the sound of weeping was muddled with the Shofar sounds. Although the Nazis came and beat those who were present, all who were there somehow felt taller after hearing the soulful sound of our faith.

Many years later, *Rebbetzin Jungreis* told this story in a small village in Samaria called Neve Aliza shortly before Rosh Hashanah. After sharing the story, one woman in the back stood up, and spoke these incredible words: "I know exactly about the Shofar you are talking about, as it was smuggled into the compound in a garbage can filled with soup. It was my father, the rabbi of the compound, who blew it. And nt only this, but my father kept the shofar ever since, and it is at our home in Neve Aliza."

She ran back home and returned with the Shofar in hand. Together, the two of them held it in their hands and wept, once two beaten little girls in Bergen Belsen, and now alive and well in Israel. It was a powerful testament to the eternal flame and triumphant spirit of the Jewish People. Hitler and Nazi Germany ended long ago, but the Jewish People continue to this day, celebrating Rosh Hashanah and blowing the Shofar.

Spiritual Exercises:

1. Try to remember a moment when you felt God's Presence in your life. What was occurring at the time? Is there anything you can do to help bring God's Presence in your life on a regular basis?

2. Take some time before Rosh Hashanah to do some introspection on the past year. Write a list of your accomplishments but also write a list of your struggles and downfalls. Try to take some time to think of ways to avoid these pitfalls so the coming year can be better. Write a list of goals that you hope to accomplish in the coming year.

3. Take time to study more about the holiday both in the days leading up to the Holiday and on the holiday itself. Learn a little more about the rituals and prayers that are done on Rosh Hashana, and their meaning and significance. Then think about how their significance can make an impact on your life.

Yom Kippur: The Power of Forgiveness

"For you are the forgiver of Israel and the Pardoner of the tribes of Jeshurun in every generation and besides You we have no King who Pardons and forgives only You my God. Before I was formed I was unworthy and now that I have been formed it is as if I had not been formed. I am dust in my life and will surely be so in my death behold before you I am like a vessel filled with shame and humiliation. May It Be Your Will, Oh Lord my God and the god of my forefathers that I not sin again and what I have sinned before you, may You cleanse with Your abundant Mercy but not through suffering or serious illness."

—Yom Kippur Prayer

I ALWAYS APPROACH YOM KIPPUR WITH so many conflicting emotions. On the one hand, I can understand its necessity. We *all* have sinned throughout the year. We all did not measure up to our true potential. We did things that we are not proud of. But is it necessary to spend an entire day focusing on how terrible we have been? To beat ourselves up (literally and figuratively) that we are just a bunch of worthless sinners? Haven't we all had enough of Jewish Shame? Isn't living and reliving shame, which is what Yom Kippur seems to be all about, just going to make us into miserable people? In short, doesn't living shamefully mean living miserably?

I believe the only way to approach Yom Kippur is to have a radically different approach to who the real "You" is, as well as a different approach to what Teshuva is. There is an unexplained phenomenon for those who don't believe in the soul. I have always asked atheists to explain it, to which I have never gotten a satisfactory answer. This unanswerable question is: Why do people feel bad when they do something wrong? This seems to be such an inborn feeling, so deeply embedded in the human psyche that I believe nearly everyone has experienced it, and most experience it on a regular basis whenever we do something wrong (The only exception being psychopaths, who I believe are built very different spiritually than everyone else, but that is a discussion that is beyond this book). In fact, when researchers approached prison inmates and asked them what they thought about the most when they were in jail, their answer startled all of them. Even more than yearning for freedom, nearly all prisoners thought about the wrongs that they did and were filled with a deep sense of shame and remorse. Even most of the hardened criminals thought about this. And what made it even more surprising was that most of them said it wasn't only because they were being punished for what they did, but because they just realized they had done something wrong! Where does this feeling, this basic human trait come from? If a human is nothing more than a sophisticated animal, why care at all if he or she did something wrong?

And here my friends, I believe we get to the root of who we are, and the root of what I believe Yom Kippur is. You see, you and I are not a body that happens to have a soul; rather *you are a soul*. A soul yearns always for refinement, a soul cannot tolerate the corrosion of character that comes with sin. This is a very radical change from much of modern day thinking, even people who believe in the existence of the soul. There are many more proofs I believe, which show just how much *soul* we really are, but that is beyond the discussion of this chapter.

And now we turn to what Yom Kippur really is all about. It is not just about confessing our guilt; it is a day of *talking to our soul*. It is getting down to the very root of who we are. We neglect the physical body on Yom Kippur because this is not who we really are. There is a part of us that is pure royalty, that knows how petty these trivial desires that we often chase, that we are so much greater and bigger than these. That part of us is our soul. And so, the day is not really a day of shame at all, but rather of *cleansing*, a day of slowly peeling away the layers of dirt and revealing the eternal beauty that is underneath.

This idea will be explained even more in the next section when we discuss the Hebrew word *Teshuvah*.

Repentance, Prayer and Charity

One of the greatest themes of the Yom Kippur prayer, and said after the "Unetaneh Tokef" prayer is that *Teshuva, Tfillah, and Tzedakah* have the power to remove any evil decree upon us. What is so special about these three actions? Many see this and take a simple, although incorrect translation of these words, *Teshuva* to mean "repentance," *Tefillah* means "prayer," and *Tzedakah* means "charity."

However, the late *Lubavitcher Rebbe* says something much more profound about these three actions. The word *Teshuvah* does not really mean "Repentance." The true word for "Repentance" would be *Charatah*, which stems from feeling ashamed for one's actions, and a willingness to change. However, *Teshuvah* means to "Return," that is, to return to the state that a person truly is. This means that a Jew's essence is goodness, his innermost nature is pure, he is seeking to return to his once natural state. This is a beautiful way to look at Yom Kippur, it is not just merely atoning for what a person once did, but rather an understanding of his or her own deepest self, namely the roots of his or her soul. This soul is connected to God and wants to cling to Him once more.

The *Rebbe* goes on to say that *Tefillah* is also a mistranslation. The true Hebrew word for "Prayer" is *Bakashah*, which means to request or beseech. *Tefillah* however, means "to attach," that is, to attach oneself to God. This again means something much larger than just asking God for our needs. It is having an understanding that when a Jew prays, he is doing much more than "making requests," rather he is communicating openly with the Divine, and building a relationship with Him. This is why Yom Kippur is all about prayer, for it is a day of just soul, a day when the purest part of ourselves just wants to cling to the Divine. A day when we just want to talk to Him the way two lovers who had been far apart from each other just want to whisper sweet loving words to each other.

Finally, the *Rebbe* turns to the third on the list, which is *Tzedakah*. Once again, this word is mistranslated as "charity" but the true word which would fit charity better is *Chessed,* since charity flows through kindness. However, the word *Tzedakah* really stems from the root word *Tzedek*, which means "Justice." What does justice have to do with charity? Once again this taps into something much larger than just charity. It taps into having a greater understanding of the world, that although we all must do our share to provide for ourselves and our families, it is ultimately He who decides who has material possessions and who does not. Therefore, this world is really owned by Him, for we are all seekers from His Creation. Justice is understanding that all the abundance we have is really a blessing from Him, and it is our duty to use this blessing to help those who were less fortunate. We are performing the most beautiful act of justice when we give our abundance to those in true need.

Of all the ideas from the *Rebbe*, this understanding of *Teshuvah, Tefillah,* and *Tzedakah* is one of my favorites. For it taps into a much greater understanding of Yom Kippur, as well as a greater understanding of what it is to be a Jew. Judaism is so deep. What we often see and hear is just the tip of the glacier. When we delve more deeply into meanings behind these texts we come to understand so much more than just the mere rituals. We come to understand why we are here, how to a certain extent the world really runs, and who we truly are. We are here to return to our once true self, to cling to God through communicating with Him, and to bring true Justice to the world through our deeds. No other creature can do this besides *Man.* Only *we* have the capacity to right that which is wrong in the world. So, on this day, we look both deeply into ourselves and outwardly into the world around us. On Yom Kippur we look at the whole world not as the way it is now, *but the way it can be.* This is Yom Kippur, and this is Jewish Living.

The Yom Kippur Moment

Yom Kippur is without a doubt the holiest day of the year. It is a day when we are stripped completely of the pleasures of physical bodies, leaving only our soul to talk to its own Maker. It is a day wrapped in prayer, wrapped in sorrow, but also wrapped in Divine Majesty. On Yom Kippur we don the white *Kittel,* the color of the angels above. Perhaps even more significantly, it is to remind us of the day when we will die, as we will all one day wear our *Kittels* in the grave, and once again stand before our Maker, stripped of our bodies with only the soul remaining. We wear our *Kittels* at times of transitions. We wear it at the *Chuppah* (wedding ceremony) when one leaves a living state of aloneness to a living state of mutual connection. We wear it on Passover night as we move from a state of slavery to freedom, subjugation to redemption. We wear it as we descend into the grave when we leave this world and enter the World to Come. And on Yom Kippur night we wear it as we leave a state of impurity and sin into a state of purity and holiness.

Yom Kippur is not truly a day of this world. It is said that the Hebrew word *HaSatan* (The Satan) has the *Gematria* (Hebrew numerical value) of 364, for Satan only has possible control over us for 364 days of the year. But that one day, Yom Kippur, he is powerless. It is a day when we can come closer to God than any other time of the year. It is, as it is written in the Torah "For through this day, He will atone for you, He will cleanse you; from all your sins before God, you will be cleansed." We enter Yom Kippur putrid and rotting with our own failures and shortcomings, we leave the day as clean and as pure as the angels above.

One of the most powerful prayers which we read both on Yom Kippur as well as Rosh Hashanah is *Unetaneh Tokef* (Let us now relate). How this prayer came into being is a miraculous story in and of itself, but that story is for another time. The prayer writes "Let us now relate the power of this day's holiness, for it is awesome and frightening. On it, Your Kingship will be exalted; Your throne will be firmed with kindness and You will sit upon it in truth. It is true that You alone are the One Who judges, proves, knows, and bears witness; Who writes and seals, Who counts and Who calculates. You will remember all that was forgotten. You will open the Book of Remembrances—it will read itself—and each person's signature is there. And the great Shofar will be sounded and a still, thin voice will be heard..." I heard once from a great teacher of mine that what is fascinating about this prayer is that even though there was a great Shofar sound, afterward a still thin voice can be heard. So often in life we go through a powerful spiritual experience, a "loud Shofar blow" so to speak. But this isn't in the end what arouses us to change, but rather it is the small inner voice that follows. Nothing is more powerful than this voice, and this voice, of course, is the voice of our soul.

I believe every one of us has at times, what I would like to call a Yom Kippur moment. This is a moment, usually during a powerful or momentous moment in our lives (but not always) when we come to the realization that God is so much a part of our lives, and the deepest purpose of our lives is to connect to Him, and we feel willing to do whatever we can to build that relationship. For some it is after a particularly moving prayer service or studying an inspiring Torah passage. For others it could be standing under the bridal canopy at their own wedding. For others it can be experiencing the birth of their child. I remember one time when I had such a moment, and it wasn't in synagogue, nor was it in the *Beit Midrash* (Torah study hall), nor was it after hearing an inspiring lecture. It happened for me when I once went with some friends on a trip to Arizona and stood at the top of the Grand Canyon. I am usually someone who, for better or for worse, likes to talk, but suddenly for perhaps the first time in my life, I was totally speechless. Standing there at the top of one of the greatest sites on earth, I could not help but reflect upon the awe of our world and its Creator. It was a moment of silence, no cell phone beeping, no cars going by, no machines beeping, and no chatter of friends. Just standing there, I felt so miniscule, so insignificant, but yet so totally alive, and so powerful. I felt the Godly spark inside of me reaching up, so to speak, and wanting to connect to Him. I felt at one with his extraordinary world, and I felt I wanted to be more at one with Him. *That*, my friends, is a Yom Kippur moment.

The Incredible Capacity to Change

Great is the human capacity to change, that nearly anyone can do it, and once it is fully done, it is as if the person has become a completely new person. Such is the power of *Teshuva*. The following well known story in the Talmud illustrates this idea well:

Eliezer Ben Dordaya had such a strong lust for women that he would seek out any prostitute, no matter how far away they lived. One prostitute lived very far away, and so he crossed seven seas to reach her.

As he began to have sexual relations with her, she realized the great lengths he had gone to meet her, and said to him "Just as a breath that comes out of me does not return, so too you will never be able to return back to God." He was so taken aback by her words, rebuke from none other than a prostitute, that he stopped the sexual act immediately and went outside. He asked for help from the mountains, the earth, the sun, and the stars and constellations. All responded that they were unable to beseech God on his behalf. Finally, he realized that the only one who could help him was himself. He put his head between his knees and cried profusely in deep remorse for his actions, cried so hard till his soul left him, and he died. A Heavenly Voice came out and proclaimed: "Great is Rabbi Eliezer Ben Dudaya, for he is ready for the World to Come." What makes the story even more significant is the fact that the Talmud called him *Rabbi*! His *Teshuva* was so complete, that not only had he become a different person, but his past became different as well. It is as if all the years of behaving poorly no longer existed. He indeed had died a fully righteous man.

A Modern Day Yom Kippur Story

There is a modern day story of Eliezer Ben Dordaya which is perhaps my favorite Holocaust story. It is the story of Schneeweiss, a self-hating secular Jew who was a brigadier for the Nazis in the Janowska Concentration Camp. One of the inmates at the camp was none other than *Rabbi Israel Spira*, the Grand Rabbi of Bluzhov. Yom Kippur day was approaching in the camp, and Rabbi Spira was given the task to request from Schneeweiss that he and other Chassidic inmates not have to perform any of the 39 forbidden labors on Yom Kippur. Incredibly, seeing the sincerity in the Rabbi's face, he complied with the request, and found chores for them on Yom Kippur day that would not violate the 39 forbidden labors. On Yom Kippur night, the beatings were particularly awful, as the Nazis knew that day was a Jewish Holiday. But still, late that night, the indominable spirit of the Jewish People prevailed, for a heartfelt, tearful *Kol Nidrei* prayer could be heard, sung by the inmates of Janowska Concentration Camp.

In the middle of the labors given to the inmates, the Nazis came in, with steaming hot food, and the camps filled with scents none of them had smelled in a long time. White bread, steaming hot vegetable soup, and large portions of meat. The Nazis, in their cruelty, wanted to order the Jews to eat, and thereby break the Yom Kippur fast. The commanding officer barked out his order "You Jews must eat immediately, or you will be shot on the spot!" No one moved.

The SS men called in Schneeweiss. "If the dirty dogs refuse to eat, I will kill you along with them." Incredibly, Schneeweiss pulled himself to attention, looked the Nazi directly in the eyes and said in a quiet but firm voice "We Jews do not eat today. Today is Yom Kippur, our most holy day, the Day of Atonement."

The Nazi Officer took out his revolver. "You don't understand, Jewish dog. I command you, in the name of the Fuhrer and the Third Reich, *fress!*"

Schnneeweis again, repeated with his head held high, "We Jews obey the law of our tradition. Today is Yom Kippur, a day of fasting." The Nazi officer pointed the gun at Schneewiess's temple. Schneeweiss remained motionless, with his head still held high. A single shot pierced the room. Schneewiess fell to the floor, with a small pool f blood gathering on the newly polished floor.

All those who witnessed this extraordinary act were in complete shock and awe. Schneeweiss, who had led his life flaunting his disbelief in Jewish tradition, had died a martyr's death, sanctifying God's great Name at the last moment. He had died with a pure soul, fulfilling the message of Yom Kippur in the most powerful way possible. A modern-day Eliezer Ben Dudaya story; he is undoubtedly sitting in the Garden of Eden alongside him for all eternity.

The message of this story is quite clear. Much like Eliezer Ben Dudaya, Schneeweiss had the capacity to change. We all do. No matter where we are now in our lives, we all have the capacity to become the next Eliezer Ben Dudaya or Schneeweiss. This capacity to change is built into us from the moment we were brought into this world. God believes in us, we need only to believe in ourselves. I bless every one of us to be able to reach within ourselves and become the greatest person we can be.

Spiritual Exercises

1. Remember a time when you did something that you knew was wrong. We all have done things that we are not proud of. How did you feel afterwards? If you felt remorse, what was the source for that feeling? Was it a physical response or did it feel spiritual?

2. Try to write a list of areas that you struggle with, and specific transgressions that you have committed. Keep this list private. But just writing it down helps to confront these areas head on.

3. Try to think of the triggers that lead to these pitfalls. Try to think of ways you can avoid these triggers so that you don't fall into the traps again. And try to identify positive behaviors that you can do that can help counteract those triggers.

4. Try to think of positive activities you can do over the course of the year to help make you into a better person. These could be anything from committing to Torah study regularly or prayer services regularly or volunteering for community needs. It could also mean committing to giving more to charity from your income. Then monitor how these activities change how you feel as a person over the year.

Sukkot: The Tabernacle of Peace

"Be seated, be seated, exalted guests; be seated, be seated, holy guests; be seated be seated, guests of faithfulness be seated in the shade of the Holy One blessed is he. Worthy is our portion Worthy is the portion of Israel as it is written "For God's portion is his people Jacob the lot of his heritage for the sake of the unification of the Holy One blessed is he and his presents to unify the name of God in perfect Unity through him who is hidden and inscrutable in the name of all Israel May the pleasantness of my Lord Our God be upon us may he established our handiwork for us our handiwork may he establish."

—Sukkot Prayer

WHEN STUDYING THE HOLIDAY OF Sukkot, the overwhelming theme is that this is a Holiday of Joy. The Torah itself writes: "You shall hold the Feast of Booths for seven days…You shall hold a festival… in the place that the Lord will choose, for the Lord your God will bless all your crops and all your undertakings, *and you shall have nothing but joy.*" In our Prayers, it often is not called by its name or the rituals we observe, it is simply called *Zman Simchatenu*, that is "The time of our Joy." In fact, the Talmud writes that there were *Simchat Beit Hashoavot*, literally meaning Rejoicing of the Water Drawing House, which took place on Sukkot. These were very festive celebrations commemorating the Water Libation ritual in the Temple each day of Sukkot. The Talmud describes the festivities in detail, from the lighting of the immense candelabrum set in the Temple courtyard (each holding gallons of oil and fit with wicks made from priests' worn-out vestments), which generated such intense light that they illuminated every courtyard in the city. A Levite orchestra of flutes, trumpets, harps, and cymbals accompanied torchlight processions, and all who had earned the capacity for real spiritual joy through their purity, character and scholarship danced ecstatically to the hand-clapping, foot-stomping, and hymn-singing crowds. The Talmud goes on to say that "one who had never witnessed the Rejoicing at the Place of the Water Drawing had never seen true joy in his life." To this day, there are great musical celebrations every night of the intermediate days of Sukkot both in Israel and the Diaspora to commemorate those Temple celebrations.

The question is, what is so joyous about this Holiday? Yes, it is certainly not a sad holiday, but many of us would probably say that Chanukah and Purim among others certainly are joyous as well, if not more joyous. So, what is unique about Sukkot that makes it so joyful? To understand the unique joy of this Holiday, we need to have a greater understanding not only of what we are celebrating, but the rituals associated with this Holiday. Let us examine each of these one by one.

The Tabernacle of Peace

The main sources for dwelling in the Sukkah is the Bible itself. Many of us know the commemoration was for the huts that our ancestors used when they were in the wilderness after the Exodus from Egypt. "Live in sukkot for seven days, so your descendants will remember that I [the Lord] had the Israelites live in wilderness shelters when I brought them out of Egypt" as the verse says. Mystics also add that it is a reminder of the *Ananei Hakavod* (Clouds of Glory) which gave the Jewish People extra protection during that time. But as we have said before, Jewish Holidays are so much more than mere commemoration. What was so special about that time in the wilderness and what is so unique about the Sukkah that we are to remember it each year by dwelling in it?

Many people overlook that really the word Sukkot was mentioned much earlier in the Torah. This was during one of our Forefather Jacob's travels. He stopped and built little huts (Sukkot) for his cattle to sleep in, and therefore the Torah writes he called the name of that place "Sukkot." How are we to understand this? What is the Torah coming to teach us with this, and what does this have to do with Jacob?

Jacob's life story was much different than his forebears. While both Abraham and Isaac lived lives of relative tranquility and honor, Jacob's entire life was one of suffering in some of the worst ways imaginable. He was deceived to work for many years for Laban, he had to run for his life from his own twin brother, his cherished wife Rachel was barren for many years, his beloved child Joseph went missing for nearly two decades. And yet the ending was one of triumph, he lived to not only be reunited with Joseph, but to see him as viceroy to all of Egypt.

Because of all of this, Jacob knew and understood well the often stormy and fleeting nature of this world, and that we have no choice but to rely on our Father in Heaven for shelter. For all his suffering, Jacob never lost his faith, for in the end, he understood God calls the shots. Jacob saw how all the seemingly loose strands fit together; Joseph went to Egypt only as second in command to none other than Pharaoh himself. Jacob, the one who struggles and succeeds, is for most of us, is the most relatable of Patriarchs. It was Jacob who dreamed of the ladder with Angels ascending and descending, going from this world to the higher world. One foot in this world but one planted firmly in the other. Often descending into the depths of this world, but still reaching for the heights of the next.

But it goes much deeper than this. Jacob not only represents this world, he represents the future Messianic world as well. For it is Jacob who struggled with the Angel of Esau all throughout the night, only defeating him at the crack of dawn. The Mystics explain this struggle to be the struggle of this world, and the dawn to be the Messianic age. Jacob, who had his named changed at that moment to *Yisrael*, for "he has struggled with the Divine (*Yisra-El*) and triumphed. Man only triumphs when God pulls back the curtain and reveals His Hand. According to Jewish tradition, it will be Jacob who is the first to greet the Messiah.

So, what does this have to do with the holiday of Sukkot? Well, everything. The Sukkah, above all else, represents the fleeting nature of this world. The Jewish People dwelt in Sukkot when they encamped in the desert. The desert more than any other place represents the difficulties of this world and our absolute reliance on Him. Moreover, Sukkot, as the Torah teaches us celebrates the beginning of the harvest and rainy season, once again reminding us just how much we need Him for all our sustenance.

So, for seven days, we leave our permanent beautiful homes and dwell in flimsy temporary dwellings. We demonstrate our Faith in Him, as Jacob did. As flimsy and painful as this world often is, we know there will one day be a Greater Day. On Sukkot we read the great prophesy of Zechariah, when all of Israel will "dwell under one Sukkah." It is the Sukkah that unifies the world.

All throughout Jewish literature we find references to the idea that a sukkah is a dwelling for both the Divine Presence and for peace in the world as well. On Shabbat we pray "Spread over us the canopy (sukkah) of your peace." Judaism has always been about peace. The word shalom is one of God's names. In biblical times they offered during the holiday of Sukkot 70 bulls which represented the 70 nations of the world, which was, in Talmudic literature, an offering of peace. But the Sukkah itself is the strongest message of peace. As we enter the Sukkah we offer a most beautiful prayer: "May it be Your Will, my God and God of my forefathers, that You cause Your presence to reside among us, that You spread over us the Sukkah of your peace."

Now we can come back and answer our original question. It is the Holiday of Sukkot which can give us the most joy. Only the holiday of Sukkot represents the totality of the Jewish story, past present and future. No other holiday represents this so well. It is the holiday commemorating what once took place when we left Egypt. It is the holiday that represents our own lives and the struggles we have. And it is the holiday that reminds us of the future days that are coming, Messianic days, days of unity and peace.

Lulav and Etrog: A Message of Unity

There is a well-known saying that every religion has rituals that are meaningful to its adherents, but to any outsider looking in, they will seem often peculiar and often ridiculous. Judaism certainly has its share of seemingly bizarre customs and laws (wearing canvas sneakers with our suit on Yom Kippur can tickle any outsider's funny bone). But perhaps none seem as bizarre as the ritual of shaking the Lulav and Etrog on Sukkot. The Torah commands us "And you shall take you on the first day the fruit of goodly trees, branches of palm-trees, and boughs of thick trees, and willows of the brook, and you shall rejoice before the Lord your God seven days." These are the four famous species which we are required to take on Sukkot, namely the Willow, the Palm Branch, the Myrtle and the Citron. During the prayers we wave them in all directions, east, west, north and south and upwards and downwards. I believe this commandment is what is called in the Torah a *Chok*, that is, a commandment for which we don't know the exact reason for. However, there are many mystical ideas that the commentators share on what the Lulav and Etrog represent. Let us examine some of these.

One of the more well-known interpretations is that the Lulav and Etrog represent parts of the human body. The *Lulav* (palm branch) represent the spine, for it is tall, thin, and straight. The *Aravot* (willow) is the shape of our mouth, the *Hadas* (myrtle) represent the eyes, and the Etrog (citron) represent the heart. Together they comprise many of the primary functions of the human body. By binding them together, we are symbolically saying that we want to use all our faculties for developing a relationship with God. And by shaking them in every direction, we are recognizing God's constant Presence in our lives, no matter which direction we turn to. And perhaps the reason why the Etrog is the one of the four singled out to have a special commandment to make it beautiful, is because the Etrog, or heart, is the seat of emotion. The most ideal way to perform a Mitzvah is with passion, for through passion we truly feel a connection to our Creator.

But perhaps the most well-known symbolism of the *Arba Minim* (Four Species) is that they represent the four different types of Jews. Taste represents learning. Smell represents good deeds. The *etrog* has both taste and smell. The *lulav* has taste but no fragrance. The myrtle has smell but no taste. And the willow has neither. Each represents a different type of man. Some have both learning and good deeds; some have good deeds but no learning; some have learning but no good deed, and some have neither. Real community is found in all these types of people being bound together and brought under one roof. I think there's a lesson in this teaching about accepting all types of people since we all make up the community of the world. This continues with the theme of Sukkot, that the Sukkah represents peace and unity.

Moreover, I believe that each one of us has experienced these four different types within our own lives. There are times in our lives when we feel inspired with both Torah and good deeds. There are times when we are drawn to one of these two but not the other. And there are times, sadly often during difficult times, when we have neither. But the message of the *Arbah Minim* is nonetheless uplifting. We can still approach God with our struggles, our daily highs and lows, and still have the opportunity to serve Him and get close to Him.

Hoshana Raba and the Seven Cycles

One of the most unusual days of the Jewish year is the final day of Sukkot, known as Hoshana Raba. There is no mention of any special significance to this day in the Written Torah, but the Holiday comes alive in Kabbalistic sources. The Zohar writes that although Judgement is sealed on Yom Kippur, it is not delivered so to speak, till Hoshana Raba. Therefore, Hoshana Raba is seen as the final opportunity for repentance. As such, extra prayers asking for salvation (*Hoshana*) are said on this day. Many people have the custom of reciting the entire book of Psalms, staying up the entire night studying Torah, or reading the book of Deuteronomy. It is also the last opportunity to recite *Tashlich*, the special prayer for repentance usually said near a riverbank.

With the understanding we said above, now it may be understandable why there is the custom to beat the *Aravah* (willow branches) on this day, at the end of the Hoshana Raba prayer to remove its leaves. The Aravah as we said before is the part of ourselves that has neither Torah or Mitzvot, the part of ourselves that we are least proud of. This ritual of Hoshana Raba thus is symbolically trying to remove this part of ourselves and return to God in purity.

One of the most beautiful customs of Hoshana Raba is the custom of walking seven rotations around the synagogue during the Hoshana Raba prayers. There are only two other rituals in Jewish tradition that involve seven rotations. This is the seven times the *Kallah* (bride) walks around her *Chattan* (groom) under the *Chupah* (wedding canopy). The other time are the seven rotations made around the synagogue during the Simchat Torah celebration. Where in the Torah do we find the concept of seven rotations, and what significance does this all have?

There is one place in the Torah where seven rotations also took place, and this is found in the book of Joshua. At the time the city of Jericho had an impenetrable wall built by its inhabitants and was thus impossible for the Jews to conquer. It is written: "The Israelites marched around the walls once every day for seven days with the priests and the Ark of the Covenant. On the seventh day they marched *seven times around the walls*, then the priests blew their ram's horns, the Israelites raised a great shout, and the walls of the city (Jericho) fell."

Before we examine the connections to these three instances, it is important to look at the significance of the number seven. Seven as we know, symbolizes a complete cycle, as there are seven "days" of creation, seven days of the week, seven years of the *Shmitah* cycle. Thus, it is the end of one cycle, and the beginning of a new one.

So now let us examine these three instances. There is a very deep connection in all three of these instances. This is symbolic of breaking down the walls which are contained within us, an end of a cycle or stage, and beginning again anew. The bride walks seven times, as she is symbolically breaking down the walls in her husband's heart, the walls which may prevent their marriage from blossoming, and thus allowing herself to enter his heart completely. When the walls are broken down, they begin anew, and the marriage can take off and soar to extraordinary heights, to the most powerful connection two humans that are not related to each other can possibly happen. And on Simchat Torah as well, the seven times continues with this theme. We all know the importance and beauty of Torah study, but so often we have created walls to prevent us from achieving true Torah greatness. These walls may be excessive pursuits in other areas that are contrary to our spiritual growth. Thus, on Simchat Torah we celebrate breaking down these walls and once again beginning anew with a new cycle of Torah study. And finally, on Hoshana Raba, we finish the *Teshuva* (repentance) cycle completely. We symbolically remove the walls contained within our own hearts that prevent us from turning to God and once again renew our commitment to God and leading a Godly life.

A Sukkot Story

There is a beautiful story found in Chassidic literature regarding a very special Etrog that I would like to share. *Rabbi Elimelech of Lizensk* was leading the services on the first day of Sukkot when he suddenly stopped, sniffed the air, and smiled radiantly. After the services were over, he walked around the synagogue and continued sniffing till he reached one simple looking Jew that was a stranger to the town holding a very simple Etrog.

"My friend," he asked this Jew. "Why does your Etrog smell like the Garden of Eden? Its beautiful scent has been permeating the entire synagogue!"

"Well," the startled man said sheepishly. "There is a story to this Etrog. I am a poor man as I am a teacher of Torah in a small town. However, I go out of my way each year to buy a beautiful Etrog, saving up as much money as I can as the holiday of Sukkot approaches. My wife helps as well, as she rents herself out as a cook before the holidays to earn some extra money.

I walk very far to a marketplace that has the most beautiful Etrogim and this year on my way I stopped at a small wayside inn. I could hear moaning and sobs coming from the inside of the inn, so I went to see what was going on. Inside, a peasant was crying and begging the innkeeper for help. It seemed his horse, his only means of livelihood, had expired near the inn, and he was begging the innkeeper if he could buy one of his horses. However, he could not afford any of them and thus was sobbing uncontrollably.

I could feel this poor Jew's pain and asked the innkeeper if I could buy one of his horses for this man. He sold me one for a very discounted price, but I needed to use up nearly all the money I had saved for the Etrog. I gave the horse to the poor Jew who thanked me profusely. I returned home and bought the simplest Etrog I could find that was still Kosher to use for the holiday. I didn't want to go to my regular synagogue as many people in my community know I always buy the most beautiful Etrog and many of them ask to make a blessing over my Etrog, and I did not want to disappoint them. So, I came here instead for the services."

Rabbi Elimelech's eyes lit up when he heard this story. "Your Etrog is indeed the most beautiful, worth far more than any Etrog you could have purchased. And I have no doubt that the poor man you met was none other than Elijah the Prophet testing you to see if you would be willing to put aside your own spiritual needs to help a fellow Jew. And you passed this extraordinary test."

I always loved the message of this story. It is a story of priorities. The greatest way to serve God has always been through helping our fellow Man, even if it means for a moment forgoing what seems to be our own spiritual growth. For in the end, although it may not seem this way, this is the greatest channel for true spiritual living.

Spiritual Exercises

1. Try to spend as much time during the Holiday of Sukkot in the Sukkah. This means not only for eating but reading and Torah study time as well. If possible, you may even try sleeping in your Sukkah as many times as you can. How does the mere act of being in the Sukkah enhance your Holiday?

2. Try to take a few minutes each day of Sukkot and appreciate the many meanings of the Holiday. This can be not only from this chapter, but from online research as well. Then monitor how your studies enhance your Holiday and your overall Judaism as well.

3. Try to purchase a Lulav and Etrog set for the Holiday and say the blessing on it each day. Try to shake the Lulav and Etrog each day according to the prescribed ritual. Spend a minute when shaking the Lulav and Etrog thinking about the symbolism of them and what shaking them means. It is a wonderful way to enhance the ritual.

4. Try to attend at least one *Simchat Beit Hashoavah* during the intermediate days of the Holiday. It is especially nice to go to one with live music and dancing. When at the *Simchat Beit Hashoavah*, try to imagine what it must have been like in the times of the Temple. Use the time to appreciate the unique joy of this Holiday.

Shemini Azeret/Simchat Torah: Torah and Water, our Life Force

"Remember the one [Moses] drawn forth in a bulrush basket from the water. They said, 'He drew water and provided the sheep with water.' At the time Your treasured people thirsted for water, he struck the rock and out came water. For the sake of his righteousness, grant abundant water!

Remember the appointee [Aaron] over the Temple, who made five immersions in the water. He went to cleanse his hands through sanctification with water. He called out and sprinkled [blood bringing] purity as with water. He remained apart from a people of water like impetuosity. For his sake, do not hold water back!

Remember the twelve tribes You caused to cross through the split waters, for whom You sweetened the water's bitter taste. Their offspring whose blood was spilt for You like water. Turn to us – for woes engulf our souls like water. For the sake of their righteousness, grant abundant water!"

—Shemini Azeret Prayer

The Mystery of Shemini Azeret

T HERE IS A HOLIDAY WHICH comes immediately after Sukkot but is still linked to the holiday of Sukkot called "Shemini Azeret." It literally means the "Eight Holiday" because it falls out eight days from the start of Sukkot. The Holiday itself is shrouded in mystery. Very little description of the holiday is contained in the Torah; it is simply written that after the seven days of the Holiday of Sukkot, we are to celebrate a day of *Azeret*, which loosely is translated as "convocation." However, the root word of *Azeret* is *Atzur*, which means "stop" or "pause." Indeed, there are no known laws prescribed in the Torah for this day, it seems to be simply a day of reflection. *Rashi* famously says in his commentary that it is as if God is telling us that He doesn't want the Holiday period to end; He wants to stay with us for one more day. What is so special about this day, which has no laws attached to it?

Interestingly, there is one Holiday in the Torah called *Azeret* as well, and this is the Holiday of *Shavuot*. The name *Shavuot,* which means "weeks," was derived later to connote the seven weeks leading up to the holiday known as the *Omer*. Insights into the *Omer* will be discussed later, in the chapter on *Shavuot*. But for now, let's study the original name that the Torah gave the holiday; namely *Azeret*. Nothing in the Torah is coincidence; these two Holidays must have had the same name because of some deep connection. What connection is there between these two holidays?

To begin to understand the answer, one must understand the cycles of the Torah, particularly the patterns of numbers. Much in the Torah centers around the number Seven, as in the "Seven Days of Creation" (whether the Biblical account of creation is meant to be taken literally or figuratively is a discussion beyond this book), the Seven Year *Shmittah* Cycle, or the Seven Fruits of the Land of Israel. The number Seven in Biblical terms typically is associated with the physical world, the natural world, so to speak. However, the number Eight often signifies something even deeper, namely that which is beyond this world. Whenever the Torah wants to commemorate or symbolize something which is beyond this world, it often uses the number eight. A baby boy is circumcised on the *eighth* day, for it signifies that he is becoming part of the Covenant of a People whose destiny is supernatural. On the holiest day of the Jewish Year, Yom Kippur, the *Kohen Gadol* (High Priest) wears *eight* garments when he walks into the Holy of Holies; as opposed to seven, which he wears during the rest of the year. And the flames of the Menorah burned for *eight* days, symbolizing the miraculous nature of *Chanukah*, that God had intervened, and the story of Chanukah was supernatural indeed.

What does this have to do with Shavuot and Shemini Azeret? It is interesting to note that Shavuot falls right *after* counting a seven-week cycle; that is right at the fiftieth day, which is the *eighth* week. It is said in the *Midrash* that the Jewish People had to ascend to the fiftieth level of purity (considered to be the highest level) to reach the level worthy enough to receive the Torah, which is of course the start of the eighth week. To receive the Divine Wisdom of the Torah, we needed to reach the fiftieth level, and reach that level of eight.

Incredibly, Shemini Azeret follows this same pattern! The only other Holiday beside Shavuot which is called by the Torah "Azeret" is also reached through the level of fifty days, which is the eighth week! The High Holiday season really begins from the first of Elul, which is thirty days before Rosh Hashanah, when the Talmud teaches that the process of *Tshuvah* (repentance) really begins. And as we discussed in the last chapter, the final day for *Tshuvah* is Hoshana Raba, the day right before Shemini Azeret! So Shemini Azeret is the next day, the 50th day, right when we begin anew, just as Shavuot, after purification for 49 days, is the 50th day. What an incredible parallel and insight into these two holidays.

The Blessing of Rain: Recognizing the Source

One of the highlights of the Shemini Azeret prayer service is the *Tefilat Geshem*, that is, the prayer for rain. Judaism places the importance of praying for rain at the very beginning of Creation. Indeed, we are told in the very beginning of Genesis that although even after vegetation and animals were created, which rely on rain for sustenance, it did not begin to rain yet till after man was created. The Talmud explains that God wanted to instill in the world the sense of understanding our dependence on Him, on our ability to beseech God for our needs through Prayer. It was only after Adam began to pray, that rain began to fall.

The Talmud writes one other fascinating aspect about rain. The Talmud writes that there are three Keys for God alone that will never be given to Man. These three Keys are Life, Resurrection of the Dead, and Rain. Indeed, with all the advancements in technology today, as we may be able to predict *when* rain will come, but we still have no control over *bringing it to rain on our own.* This truly is a Key which is only in God's Hands.

And so, the blessing of rain is of major prominence throughout the Bible and Talmud. Arguably in the most important prayer that we are obligated to say twice a day, the *Shema*, we recite the portion from Deuteronomy which discusses the rewards for observing God's *Mitzvot* (commandments) "I will give the rain of your land in its time." In the blessing asking for *Parnassa* (livelihood) which we say 3 times a day in the Amida, we beseech God to allow it to rain, as rain is very much an integral part for many of our livelihoods, even in today's day and age. Even though many associate the importance of rain only for farmers, the rain effects many other things as well.

So why is the holiday of Shemini Azeret chosen as the holiday to say the prayer for rain? The simple answer is that Shemini Azeret falls right around the beginning of the fall season; which is when rainy season begins. As such, it is an ideal time to begin asking for rain.

However, I believe there may be another reason why we say this prayer. As we mentioned before, there is another powerful aspect to Shemini Azeret, namely that it is also Simchat Torah, the day that we celebrate completing the Torah. What does Torah have to do with rain?

The Torah in numerous places is compared to rain. One of the most well-known verses is in Deuteronomy where it is written "May My teachings descend like rain." How is Torah compared to rain? The Talmud says that just as water flows from a higher place to a lower place; i.e. water flows downward, so too Torah can only descend from a higher place to a lower place (i.e. one can only acquire it with humility.)

However, I believe there is a much deeper connection between Torah and water. In Judaism, there are very strong correlations between the Body and Soul. Both are deeply woven within the very fabric of a human being. Just as the Body needs nourishment, so too the Soul needs nourishment. And so just as water is the Body's main source of nourishment, so too the Torah is the soul's main source of nourishment.

We see this idea most succinctly in a parable given by the great Talmudic sage Rabbi Akiva. Rabbi Akiva lived at a time when studying Torah was forbidden by the Romans. Nevertheless, he continued to study and teach Torah regularly. One day, he was approached by one of his colleagues and asked why he continued to study even though the price for Torah study meant imprisonment and possible death. He answered with a remarkable parable:

A fox once sees a fish swimming away from a fisherman's net. The fox slyly asks the fish, "Why are you swimming away from the net? Why don't you just come up onto dry land where you will be safe?" The fish, seeing through the fox's bait, retorts, "Here in the water, which is the only place we can live, it is dangerous for us, how much more so, on dry land, where we cannot even live!"

Rabbi Akiva explained that this is how it is for the Torah. The Torah itself writes that Torah, what water is for a fish, is our lifeblood, and it is essential to our Jewish survival. How much more so, we cannot survive without it. It is worth taking some risk with its study, even if it means we must avoid the fisherman's net which is the Roman Empire.

It is no coincidence that it is water which changed Rabbi Akiva's life. He was an ignoramus who hated religious people until he was 40 years old. One day Rabbi Akiva saw water dripping onto a rock. He could see that over the years the water had penetrated the Rock and had made a small opening in it. He said to himself that perhaps the Torah which is compared to water can penetrate "The Rock" which is my own heart. And so, at the age of 40 he began to study Torah. And soon he became a legend, an icon of the Talmud, a giant of a man who had amassed over 24,000 students. This idea of Torah being able to penetrate our own hearts will be discussed more in the next section.

Simchat Torah: The Inner Circle

Undoubtedly, one of the most joyous days of the Jewish calendar is Simchat Torah. It is the time of the year when we finish reading the weekly Torah portion. There are many customs for the day. Some of my favorites are the special blessing known as *Kol Hanearim* (All of the Children), the custom to give an *Aliyah* to every member in the synagogue, and the custom of dancing seven rotations around the synagogue. I would like to discuss each in a little more detail, and some of their significance to me.

The custom of *Kol Hanearim* is to call up all the children in the synagogue and read a section of the Torah with all the children under one or several *talesim* (prayer shawls). It concludes with the blessing of *Hamalach Hagoel*, (May the Angel Redeem) the final blessing which Jacob imparted to his grandchildren before he died. This prayer is especially meaningful because it emphasizes the importance of our children in the continuity of Torah and Jewish tradition. The *Shema*, arguably the most important prayer in the entire Siddur (prayer book), emphasizes the importance of imparting the Torah to our children. "And you shall teach this (Torah) to your children, and recite these words, when you arise and when you go to sleep" as the Torah says. Perhaps nothing is more important than *Mesorah*, that is the handing over of Judaism to the next generation.

Another beautiful custom is to give every male in the synagogue an Aliyah. This custom helps to emphasize that the Torah can be both relevant and meaningful to every single Jew. There was a teaching from *Reb Mendel of Kotsk*. He used to say that a man can stand under the wedding canopy and say a hundred times *"Harei At Mekudeshet, Harei At Mekudeshet"* (Behold you are betrothed) but it won't mean anything until he adds the word *Li* (To me). Until he makes the wedding vow personal, that is he makes it to himself, only then does the marriage ceremony become valid. So too, he explains, it is with the Torah. One can study Torah as just intellectual pursuit, but it only becomes real and meaningful once a person internalizes it. This is the message of each person getting an Aliyah. It is a chance to remember that the Torah can help each person with their own unique challenges th reach their spiritual potential.

And finally, we turn to in my opinion, the greatest custom of all, and this is the seven *Hakafot* (rotations) around the synagogue that we do with dancing. As mentioned before in the section on Hoshana Raba, the number seven has great significance as it symbolizes the number of times the Jewish People encircled the city of *Yericho* (Jericho) before its impenetrable walls collapsed. This I believe is to remind us that the Torah also can remove the walls contained within us. We are coming around full circle again to the story of Rabbi Akiva. He discovered that the Torah, which is compared to water, can penetrate the rock which was his heart, much as water can eventually penetrate a physical rock.

We all have our own spiritual obstacles. Some are self-inflicted, such as pursuing desires which are contrary to our own spiritual well-being. Others are thrown upon us by life circumstances, such as financial or physical hardships. But either way, the message of Simchat Torah is that we all can break through these challenges. The Torah is our guide, it is our comforting Hand on our shoulder, it is the Book to give our life direction and purpose. One only must seek, to explore its timeless wisdom, and one will begin to see the Torah break down these barriers. I bless each of us to experience the Torah as it can be for each of us, a source of comfort and meaning, a timeless guide to help us reach our own spiritual potential.

A Simchat Torah Story

The story is told about the great *Rabbi Moshe Leib Sossever*. All over the Jewish community, Chassidim would come on Simchat Torah to see the great Rabbi Moshe Leib Sossever dance with the Torah scroll. One Simchat Torah, he was nowhere to be found. As the clock ticked and the hour got late for the morning services, people in the synagogue assumed he must have been sick and so the services went on without him.

However, a few Chassidim decided to walk to his house and see what had happened to him. On the way, they passed a home where they could hear singing. They peeked inside the windows and were amazed with what they saw. They saw the great Rabbi Moshe Leib Sossever, with his face glowing radiantly, singing and dancing around a little boy in a wheelchair. The boy had a look of joy on his face that was nothing like the Chassidim had ever seen before.

Afterwards, they went to ask Rabbi Moshe Leib what had happened. He told them that he was on the way to the synagogue that morning when he heard crying coming out of this home. He went inside and saw this little boy weeping uncontrollably. He asked the boy what was wrong, and the boy responded that his parents had gone off to the synagogue to see the great Rabbi Moshe Leib Sossever sing and dance with the Torah scroll. However, they had left him at home since he was a cripple and would not be able to go that far. So, Rabbi Moshe Leib decided to drop his plans of going to the synagogue and instead sing and dance all seven *Hakafot* (rotations) around this one little boy.

I always loved this story for its message. Rabbi Moshe Leib understood what true Torah living really is. To him, it was more important to sing and dance for one little crippled boy who badly needed it, than to sing and dance for all his Chassidim in a public spectacle. It is often about putting aside one's own spiritual needs to help another person in need. That Simchat Torah was undoubtedly the greatest Simchat Torah that Rabbi Moshe had ever had.

Spiritual Exercises

1. Try to think of some of the barriers that prevent you from spiritual growth. How have those barriers affected your life? What do you feel can be done to remove those barriers?

2. Try to look in the Torah for wisdom on ways to remove these obstacles. The Torah is so vast and deep, it has something to say about every subject. Try to find areas of Torah that speak to you, and hep you grow. Try to find a *Chavrusa* (study partner) so that you can explore it together.

3. Try to partake in a Simchat Torah celebration. Sing and dance as many of the *Hakafot* as you can and participate in the services. The singing and dancing can help you become more enthusiastic about appreciating the Torah and studying it.

Chanukah:
Shattering Darkness with Light

"We light these lights for the miracles and the wonders,

For the redemption and the battles that you made for our forefathers

In those days at this season, through your holy priests.

During all eight days of Chanukah these lights are sacred

And we are not permitted to make ordinary use of them,

But only to look at them; in order to express thanks

And praise to Your great Name for your miracles, Your wonders

And your salvations."

—Jewish Chanukah Prayer

CHANUKAH IS BEAUTIFUL. THERE IS little argument with this one. Every Jew feels a sense of magic in the air, a child-like sense of wonder. Moreover, Chanukah, probably above all other Holidays, captures our imagination. It is a time of family, warmth, singing, latkes, parties, gifts, and of course, lighting the Menorah. Everyone for a moment feels proud to be Jewish, as we bask in the glow of lights, lights which have been lit for thousands of years; lights which have been lit by our parents and our grandparents.

But Judaism is much more than about just maintaining tradition. Yes tradition is important, but Judaism goes so much deeper than that. To really grasp the full meaning and depth we need to examine both the story of Chanukah and what these lights really represent.

Ah, the story of Chanukah. We know this story so well; it is so deeply embedded into our psyche. Our parents may have told us the story when we were very little. But therein lies part of the problem; we so often look at these stories with the same simplicity as we did when we were children. Part of looking at the story from a young child's perspective is wonderful, but a child does not yet fully grasp all of the nuances and hidden meanings within the story. So now, as adults, the story very much bears repeating.

So for a moment, let us flash back to the Chanukah story. Before 168 BCE, the Jews were ruled by the Seleucids (Greek-Syrians), but had relative religious autonomy. The Jewish situation changed dramatically when Antiochus IV took over as the Emperor of the Syrian country. In the year 168 BCE, the Greek-Syrian army massacred thousands of Jews, grabbed hold of the Jewish Temple, and erected a statue of the Greek god Zeus, demanding all Jews bow to it. In addition, he outlawed practicing the Jewish religion and demanded that Jews recognize the Greek Gods. In particular, the Talmud says he put a ban on circumcision, Torah study, and blessing the new moon. Many of the Jews at the time fell prey to Hellenism, an assimilation into Greek culture, and abandoned their Jewish Faith and traditions.

One day Antiochus's men erected an altar in the marketplace of Modiin, and ordered a pig to be sacrificed by the Jews to the Greek gods. Mattityahu, the High Priest, refused, crying out that he will never abandon the covenant made by his forefathers. When another Hellenistic man stepped forward to perform the sacrifice, Mattityahu pulled out a sword and killed the man before he had a chance to offer the sacrifice. Mattityahu and his followers killed many of the Greek soldiers who were there, and the rest fled.

Inspired, Mattityahu together with his son Yehuda (Judah) began to organize a small but courageous group called the Maccabees. The acronym for the Maccabees is the Hebrew letters Mem, Cuf, Beit, and Hay. These letters stand for "Mi Camocha Ba-Elim Hashem," which means, "Who is like You from the gods, but You, God!"

A lot of understanding the "hidden story" of Chanukah lies in looking at how it is celebrated today. While there are some well-known customs such as eating oily foods (latkes, fried jelly doughnuts known as *sufganiot,* and spinning the dreidel) the most well-known is of course the lighting of the Menorah. In fact, this is the only real Mitzvah or commandment pecific to the Holiday. The only other ones are related specifically to the prayer service, such as the addition of *Hallel.* So obviously the lighting of the Menorah is the most important aspect to the Holiday itself.

Lighting candles is certainly a beautiful and inspiring act. We bring in and escort out Shabbat with candles. There is so much warmth and light that a little flame can provide. But it is deeper than this. There is a well-known verse in the Book of Proverbs *"Ner Hashem Nishmat Adam,"* which means "The candle of God is the soul of Man." What does this mean? The analogy is comparing Man to a candle. A candle as we know has two components; namely the candle which holds the wick, and the flame itself. Each person as we know is comprised of both a body and a soul. The body is the physical part of us, similar to the candle, and the soul which is the flame. The body serves to house the soul, much like the candle serves to house the flame. The verse is saying that God has implanted into each and every one of us a Candle, that is, a part inside each of us to hold the Divine Essence itself. But we need to find that candle and ignite the spark, by doing deeds to bring Godliness into the world. By bringing Godliness into the world, we are in reality using the candle God has given us, using the Soul for its true purpose.

So what does this have to do with Chanukah? With a deeper understanding of the Chanukah story, we can understand very well the connection. What was taking place at the time of the Chanukah story wasn't only about a small group of Jews battling the mighty Greek Empire. It was much more than that. It was an ideological battle of monumental importance. The Greeks as many of us know represent "Beauty" and "Wisdom," but only beauty and wisdom as it relates to the physical world. The Greeks were the largest culture on the world stage to celebrate worship of the body. The Body was the Greek Temple. The strong physique was the symbol of true power, which was often personified in the Gladiator. Wisdom was used primarily to further the advance of the body such as building the great coliseums for further entertainment. The Jewish People were the complete opposite of this. The Jew represents a worship not of the body, but of the soul, the body is just the shell, or vessel to contain the Divine Light that is the Human Soul. This is the reason that the Greeks were persecuting Jewish worship so strongly, it diametrically opposed everything they stood for and believed in. In fact, the three *Mitzvot* that the Greeks banned were the Sabbath, Circumcision, and Sanctifying the New Moon each month. Why specifically these three? Perhaps because all three of these were ways to elevate physicality to a higher place. The Sabbath is a day of rest, but mainly a spiritual rest, a day of man relinquishing his mastery over nature. The specific Sabbath laws are all designed to allow us an opportunity to remember and reflect on God's sovereignty over us, of our Higher Purpose. When we sanctify the New Moon, we are saying that God has given us the ability to sanctify time; that time is precious, and only man has the opportunity each month for renewal. And finally, circumcision, when we make an indelible mark on our own bodies, by saying that our own bodies can be a vessel to create holiness in the world. So the battle with the Greeks wasn't just about sovereignty over Jerusalem and the Temple, it was an ideological battle about purpose and meaning. This is why the holiday surrounds the ritual of lighting a candle, for the candle is what the Jew represents, and displays our triumph over Greek philosophy, indeed a triumph of the soul. It is for this reason that so much emphasis is placed on the miracle of the oil burning even though many would argue that the greater miracle was the military victory of a small group of Maccabees being able to drive the mighty Greek Empire out of Jerusalem. It is because the candle and what it represents is the real underlying miracle of the Chanukah story.

It is therefore no coincidence that so much of the Jewish story as well as Jewish ritual is surrounded by fire. The Jewish People began when Abraham offered a sacrificial lamb to God in his son Isaac's stead, a sacrifice made through fire. It is from a burning bush that God first spoke to Moses. The fire was a bush that was burning, but was not being consumed, hinting to the spiritual nature that fire has. The Torah was given at Mount Sinai amidst fire in the greatest Divine Revelation man has ever seen. Indeed the Torah is even compared to fire as it is written in the verse "Behold these words are like fire, says God." And each week we bring the Sabbath in with fire when we light Sabbath candles and the Sabbath leaves when the fire of the Havdalah candle is extinguished.

Nothing in Judaism is mere coincidence, as we see from the Chanukah story there is such deeper meaning behind fire and what it represents for us. The significance of the Chanukah candle can even be seen in the Jewish laws that surround it, as we will see in the next section.

The Inner Beauty of Chanukah's Laws

Many people believe that *Halacha*, or Jewish Law are just arbitrary laws made by man that have almost no bearing on the Holiday itself. Indeed, nothing can be further from the truth. Often the Laws are designed to bring out deeper spiritual truths contained in the holiday itself. Perhaps in no other holiday do we see this most acutely as we do in the holiday of Chanukah. Chanukah's laws and customs are laden with depth and meaning. There are numerous examples of this. Let us examine a few of them.

According to Jewish Law, one should not use the light of the Chanukah candle for any other purpose. For example one should not use the lit Chanukah candles as reading light. The only use we can have for the light is to stare at the light itself! Once again, we see the deeper meaning of the light, as we discussed above. If the Chanukah light was just there as mere commemoration, then it would not make much difference what we use the light for, once it is lit. But if we understand that the light serves a Higher Purpose, to awaken the spirit and soul within us, to remind us of the spiritual nature of light, then using that light for any profane purpose diminishes the essence of what the candles are. Furthermore, one should not, according to Jewish Law, be involved in work-related activities while the candles are burning. Again, we see this theme of the holiness of these lights. The time when the candles are burning is very sacred and anything to diminish that is diminishing the Holiday itself.

One of the most well-known laws is that the ideal oil which should be used for the *Mitzvah* is olive oil, for that is what was used in the Temple at the time of the Chanukah story. But I believe it goes much deeper than that. It is a well-established fact that olive oil is the purest form of oil, the highest quality. At the time of the Chanukah story, the

Jews were only able to find one small jug of oil which still was untouched and had the seal of the *Kohen Gadol*, the High Priest. *Rabbi Abraham Isaac Kook* says that this jug of olive oil symbolizes the purity contained deep within every Jew which cannot be broken and still has the seal on it, untarnished by the false ideologies and influences. On Chanukah we are symbolically finding that little jug within each of us, and igniting it, bringing it back to life.

It is interesting to note that the word *Shemona* which means "eight" has the same root letters as the word *Neshama*, which means "soul." The number eight, that is, the number of the nights of Chanukah, is known in Judaism to transcend nature, just as the soul transcends the body. This is why a boy is circumcised on the eighth day, for it symbolizes that the covenant of the Jewish People for which he joins transcends nature. And so with the story of Chanukah and all it represents, is the story of the transcendence of the Jewish People. Even more compelling is that the Hebrew word for oil is *Shemen*, which also contains the root letters for *Neshama*. This is as Rabbi Kook explained above, that the purest form of oil, that is olive oil, represents the Jewish soul. It is by no coincidence that according to our tradition, Jewish Kings were anointed with oil, as part of the inauguration process, for it is to help instill in them a sense of purity and sincerity when they embark on the great task of ruling over Israel.

Another law is that we light the candles going up in number instead of going down, meaning we go from one to eight, instead of going from eight to one. This was actually a subject of dispute in the Talmud between the great sages Hillel and Shamai. Shamai said that we are to count down, that is from eight to one, but Hillel said we are to count up, that is from one to eight. We follow the ruling of Hillel; that is we count from one to eight. Why is this? I believe that the answer is since a Jew is always supposed to ascend in holiness, never descend, so we count up, never down. It is similar, I believe, to why we count up in numbers in regard to *Sefira*, the period leading up to the holiday of Shavuot. We count up to 50, since we are ascending spiritual levels to reach Mount Sinai. Life is all about growth, about reaching greater heights than where we were before.

Another significant law is that the ideal place for lighting candles is where they can be seen publicly. The most common reason given for this is *Pirsumei Nissah,* or "publicizing the miracle." I believe it goes much deeper than this. The Jewish People, as we know, are given the task to be an *Ohr Lagoyim,* or "a light onto the nations." Unfortunately, there is much darkness in the world, and our task is to bring light to the darkest of places. Lighting the menorah publicly goes beyond merely publicizing the miracle, it tells the Jewish People's story, it tells our mission.

The Indomitable Power of the Jewish Spirit

We all know that Chanukah is celebrated for eight days to commemorate the miracle of Chanukah. The miracle was that that they only had enough oil to burn for one day, but yet the oil burned for eight days, which was enough time to receive the special oil that was used for the Temple. There is a well-known question; why then do we celebrate the holiday for eight days when the miracle was in reality only seven days, since the first day was not a miracle? After all, according to natural law they had enough oil to burn for one day, so why celebrate that first day? There are many answers to this question, the most well-known one was that it was a miracle that they were able to find even that one jug of oil, since the Temple had been ransacked and defiled so terribly. However, I once heard a beautiful answer from *Rabbi Binny Friedman* in Israel. He said that the miracle of that first day *was that Jews still wanted to light the Menorah!* After being persecuted for so long by the Greeks, being forbidden to practice Judaism, Jews still were able to find it in their hearts to want to light, to practice their faith. This is the secret power of the Jewish soul, to always want to serve God and get close to Him, despite impossible circumstances.

A Modern-Day Chanukah Story

I once read an incredible story from *Yaffa Eliach* in her well-known classic *Hasidic Tales of the Holocaust.* The story is about the saintly Rabbi Yisrael Singer, known as the Bluzheve Rebbe. The year was 1943 and the place was hell on earth; the Bergen Belsen Concentration Camp. It was the first night of Chanukah, and somehow some of the Jewish prisoners had managed to use a wooden clog as a wick holder and some shoe polish as oil. A few shreds of thread from one of the prisoner's garments were wound together to form a wick.

Despite the fact that being caught participating in lighting the Chanukah candle would mean certain death, nevertheless a small crowd of beaten sunken emaciated inmates gathered around Rabbi Singer late that night. Rabbi Singer slowly began to recite the blessings over the Chanukah candles in a voice that trembled with emotion, first saying the blessing for the commandment to light candles and then saying the blessing over the miracle of the Chanukah story. When he came to the third blessing, which thanks God for being alive to see and experience this moment, he paused and looked around, before concluding the blessing.

A secular Jew who was involved in Jewish leadership in Warsaw afterwards remarked to the Rabbi "Rabbi, I understand how you were able to make the first two blessings. But how were you able to have the *chutzpah* to say the third blessing? Can you really say such words here in a place where you see the entire world burning around you? Your own people, including yourself, being systematically tortured, starved, and butchered? Can you really thank God for "sustaining you to be alive for this moment"?

The rabbi responded "Yes, you are 100 percent right. I too, wondered if I was even allowed to say such a blessing. I turned around to ask one of the other rabbis who was here and was absolutely astounded by what I saw. I saw a hundred faces that were beaten, but yet were looking up at me eagerly, thirsty to hear the blessing. When I saw this, I really did feel it was appropriate to make such a blessing. I felt at that moment what a privilege it was to be part of such a special people."

It is our tenacity, our courage, and our faith that is not only the secret of the Chanukah story, but the secret of our People as well. Being chosen doesn't only mean being given a specific mission in life, it means being willing to strive to fulfill that mission no matter how difficult it may be.

Picking Up the Broken Pieces

There is another beautiful Chanukah story that took place about 100 years ago. The story is about a poor Rabbi who once travelled to Italy to collect money for his family. While he was there, he met a very wealthy Jew who invited him to spend the Sabbath with him. While he was there, he saw a closet filled with exquisite glass, silverware, and other priceless collectibles. However, one vessel stood out in the closet; a simple broken flask that had been glued together with pieces of glass still jutting out from it.

Curious, the poor rabbi asked the wealthy owner why he had such an ugly broken piece amongst such other beautiful items. The wealthy man explained to him the following story: He had been brought up in a traditionally religious family. However, when he moved to Italy to help his family business, he became extremely successful, and little by little began to abandon Judaism. As he got caught up in the whirlwind of the business life, he began observing Judaism less and less till eventually he and his family abandoned it all together.

One day, as he was walking home from work, he saw a child crying bitterly, and the child kept moaning to himself "What will I tell my father? What will I tell my father?" He asked the boy what was wrong. The boy explained his father had saved a few gold coins to buy a little flask of oil since tonight was the first night of Chanukah. His father had sent him to go buy it and instructed him not to play with his friends on the way home since the flask may break. On the way home, he disobeyed his father and stopped to play with his friends, and indeed the flask broke. The little boy pointed to the broken flask lying on the floor.

The wealthy businessman right away consoled the boy and went to the store and bought a new, more beautiful flask for the boy to take home. But afterwards, as he returned home, the boy's words began to echo in his mind "What will my father say?" He began to see a Divine sign in this message, "What will my Father say? My Father in Heaven who has given me a task to develop a relationship with Him through the Mitzvot, and I have abandoned Him?" He immediately went back to the same spot where the boy was, and picked up the broken pieces and brought them home. That night, he surrounded his family around the table and announced that they would light the first candle that night for Chanukah, something he hadn't done in years. And the next night he lit a second candle. And the third night, he lit a third candle. It went on for the entire eight days. And that began his gradual return to Judaism. He always kept that flask as a reminder that he once had to see a broken flask to remind him how broken he was.

In a sense, we are all broken flasks. We all go through difficult times when we wander away from our true selves. Chanukah, which comes every year at the coldest time of the year, when the nights are longest, is here to remind us that we too have the ability to pick up the broken pieces of the flask. And light the candles, and once again begin anew.

Spiritual Exercises

1. Try to remember when you were inspired by candlelight. When was it? What made you feel inspired during that moment? Try to take a few moments each night of Chanukah and re-experience that same feeling.

2. Think about the story of Chanukah, all of the aspects, the military victory, the miracle of the oil, etc. Which part of the story speaks to you the most and why? See if you can find ways to enhance your own life through the message of the Chanukah story.

3. Spend a few minutes each night singing and dancing next to the Chanukah candles when they are lit. If you are not familiar with any Chanukah songs, go online and find some Chanukah songs that you enjoy. See how much this simple act of song and dance inspires the Holiday for you.

4. Spend at least one night of Chanukah lighting together with family or friends. Try to make a Chanukah party and do more than just have good food. Have some Chanukah music playing and share some inspiring words about the holiday at the party. Chanukah parties are great, but they can be made even more wonderful when they are made a little bit meaningful as well.

Tu B'shvat: A Celebration of Earth

"Look at My works, see how beautiful and wondrous they are! For your sake I created them all. See to it that you do not spoil and destroy My world; for if you do, there will be no one else to repair it."

—Midrash Ecclesiastes

THERE IS A SAD MISCONCEPTION when it comes to Judaism and the environment. Many people believe Judaism, and therefore by extension, Jews, do not care very much for the environment and the preservation of the world we live in. They believe that traditional Jews are mostly concerned with preserving Jewish law and ritual, and maybe, some of the better ones, are also concerned with caring for their neighbor's well-being. However, caring for the environment? That was for the "crazy Green Peace people," or the "Hippies who like to hug trees." But Judaism? Judaism has nothing to do with that.

I used to believe this myself. I never bothered recycling, never thought twice about littering, and didn't care much about pollution. Judaism, I thought, never really concerns itself with such petty things. Sure, I knew about *Tikun Olam,* the Jewish concept of Fixing the World, which we speak of 3 times a day when we pray, but this, I believed, was only referring to helping our fellow Man to make the world a better place.

All of this changed when I visited the beautiful Stalactite Cave in Israel. Considered by many to be Israel's greatest natural wonder, I, as an avid lover of nature, was eager to go to such a site. It was there, that I saw the quote from the Midrash above at the beginning of this chapter, right at the entrance to the cave. The quote does not mince words; it gives man the task of caring for our world, there is no one else to care for it. As I walked through that cave (and yes, it certainly *did* live up to its reputation for unparalleled beauty and exquisite rock formations) I began to think very deeply about this quote. Does God really care about us preserving his world? Is this indeed a Jewish task?

The more I began to explore this question, the more I began to see that not only does God care about us preserving His world, it is one of the fundamentals of the Torah, discussed at the very beginning of the Bible. In fact, the Bible begins with the creation of the world, not the creation of Man. Whether the Biblical account of Creation was meant to be taken literally or figuratively is a discussion beyond this book. However, the fact that the Bible begins with the creation of the world and not with creation of Man I believe is there to teach us about Man's responsibility to the earth we live in. Indeed at the very beginning of Genesis, Man is placed in the Garden and commanded to "tend to it and watch over it." Man at the very beginning was commanded to "master" the Land. Mastering means harnessing the great powers that the Land contains, but also not getting arrogant and diminishing the land by ignoring its own needs. There is even a commandment in the Torah against *Baal Tashchit*, which means letting things go to waste. We are obligated to preserve our world as best as we can. We are also given a commandment to say a special blessing in the Hebrew month of Nissan, the beginning of the spring, when we first see trees beginning to bloom. God wants us to appreciate His world, and to use it as a way to draw closer to Him.

What does this all have to do with Tu B'shvat? Well, in a very real way, it has everything to do with Tu B'shvat. Tu B'shvat is a great but often overlooked Holiday that isn't mentioned in the Bible, and is only given brief mention in the Talmud. In Tractate Rosh Hashanah it is called "the Rosh Hashanah (New Year) for Trees." However, no commandments are mentioned regarding the day. The only universal custom we have associated with that day is to eat a "new" or exotic fruit, a fruit that we do not typically eat throughout the year. We say a special blessing on this fruit, a *Shehechianu*, which is a blessing we say on special and rare occurrences.

However, in Kabalistic literature, the Holiday of Tu B'shvat explodes with prominence. In Kabbalah we find the concept of the Tu B'shvat Seder, which is a unique experience which centers around exotic fruits and around the seven special fruits of the land of Israel that the Torah speaks about. This Seder is filled with mystical blessings and chants as well as drinking four cups of wine, similar to what is done on Passover. The four cups even turn gradually from white wine to red wine, much like the four seasons change, with white representing winter, and red representing spring. There are many online resources for how to conduct a Tu B'shvat Seder for those who are interested in conducting this sacred ritual.

However, there is one aspect of Tu B'shvat which is discussed in the Seder that gets to the heart of what Tu B'shvat is. It is on this day that Kabalah writes one of the greatest "fixings" takes place; that Tu B'shvat is to fix the sin of Adam and Eve eating from the Tree. How are we to understand this? What connection does Tu B'shvat have to the sin of Adam and Eve? And how can Tu B'shvat repent for this?

There are numerous interpretations given to the story of Adam and Eve, and many commentators do not take the story literally. But what nearly all commentators agree on is that on some level, Adam and Eve's great Sin was that they partook of the Earth in a way that was not meant to be taken of. They had disobeyed God's word, which was not to eat the "fruit" of the Tree of Knowledge of Good and Evil. (Whether the "fruit" was literal or not is a long discussion amongst commentators). And on some level, the commentators explain, Adam and Eve believed that by eating of this fruit, they would become all powerful beings and have Divine Wisdom, greater or equal to God Himself. This is as it is written in the verse, when the "snake" tempted Eve. (Snake again is unclear if it was literal or perhaps a representation of the Evil Inclination). The snake said to her "If you eat from the fruit it will open your eyes, and you will be like God, knowing Good and Evil." The snake was promising that the fruit would bring eternal wisdom, and would make Man omniscient.

This is using the earth the wrong way. This is Man's arrogance, when Man isn't using the earth to better himself, it is Man manipulating the earth to serve his own selfish desires. When Man disregards what the earth is to be used for, he becomes in some ways, even lower than the earth itself.

This is what Tu B'shvat comes to fix. Here we are utilizing fruit for the way it is intended to be used, to draw ourselves closer to God and appreciate His world. To bring the earth around us to its higher purpose.

It is interesting to note that Man is compared to a tree, as the verse writes "A person is like the tree of a field." The Torah as well is even compared to a tree as the well-known verse says "It is a Tree of Life for all those who grasp it." A tree is all about potential. It needs to be watered, tended to, and it needs the proper sunlight and nutrients from the ground in order for it to grow. But once it is cared for, not only does a tree grow into something beautiful that can provide nourishment and shade, it also has the potential to create other trees from its seed. But if left alone, it will wither and die. This is a powerful analogy and lies at the crux of what Tu B'shvat represents. By emphasizing that it is the New Year for Trees, it helps us to focus on our own potential, to correct our own mistakes, as well as potential to use our earth in the way that it was meant to be used.

A Tu B'shvat Story

A story is told about a simple *Melamed* (teacher of Torah) who lived in the countryside. Most of his students were hardheaded kids who would rather be playing outdoors then sitting in his classroom studying Torah. All throughout the year he grumbled at the difficulties of teaching his students and how unappreciative they were of Torah wisdom. At times he bemoaned his job as a teacher, for he felt he was wasting his time on ungrateful brats.

On Tu B'shvat the school was closed, and so one year he decided to take a walk through the nearby woods. He was hoping to see some beautiful trees and be able to appreciate Tu B'shvat more, but that year the winter was particularly harsh, and all that he saw was barren frozen trees caked in ice, completely bereft of any signs of life.

Suddenly he began to wonder, what do the trees think about and feel on Tu B'shvat? Are they aware that it is their New Year? Do they "pray" on this day as Jews do on Rosh Hashanah to have a fruitful new year? He closed his eyes, deep in thought, as he contemplated this.

When he opened his eyes, suddenly the entire forest had changed. He could see all the trees in all their shimmering beauty, with vibrant colorful leaves swaying gently to the rhythm of the breeze. He could see the uniqueness in each tree, and its incredible potential once winter had left, and spring has come. The grass beneath his feet was a dark and robust green, without a speck of snow to be seen.

Once more he closed his eyes. This time when he opened his eyes, the coldness and scarcity of winter had returned. The trees once again mere skeletons of what they once were. The snow had returned, and the grass and leaves had left again.

The Melamed returned home, but this time he was a very different person than he was before. He understood the great lesson that the trees on Tu B'shvat had taught him. Now he was able to see the beauty in each student and appreciate their own unique potential. He continued teaching his students with a completely new vigor, and indeed his students flourished and became great Torah scholars.

I bless everyone to celebrate Tu B'shvat each year the way it was meant to be celebrated, for self-growth, to appreciate and preserve the beautiful world we live in, and to be able to see the potential in ourselves as the trees expressed that day.

Spiritual Exercises

1. Try to remember a time in your life when you saw something in nature and felt God's Presence there. What made you feel connected to God then?

2. Try to make Tu B'Shvat a little more meaningful each year. Study a little about a Tu B'shvat Seder and try to conduct one if possible. If that is too difficult, buy some exotic fruits and say the special "Shehechiyanu" blessing on it.

3. Try to think of some ways you can help the environment, such as by recycling more often, littering less than before, or polluting less. Remember that this is a Jewish value.

4. Try to take a few minutes each day outside and appreciate God's world. One does not need to be standing at the top of the Grand Canyon to appreciate the beauty in the world. Even seeing a simple flower, a nice sunset, or freshly fallen snow can help one to appreciate the beautiful world we live in.

Purim: The Story of Masks and Revelations

"In the Days of Mordechai and Esther, in Shushan, the capital, when Haman, the wicked, rose up against them and sought to destroy, to slay, and to exterminate all the Jews, young and old, infants and women, on the same day, on the thirteenth of the twelfth month, which is the month of Adar, and to plunder their possessions; But You, in Your abundant mercy, nullified his counsel and frustrated his intention and caused his design to return upon his own head and they hanged him and his sons on the gallows."

-Purim Prayer

AH, PURIM. PERHAPS THE MOST beautiful and fun holiday of all. It is the day when everyone wants to be Jewish and everyone wants to participate. I remember my year in Israel, Purim was an extraordinary sight to behold. Everyone would get into the spirit of the holiday, music and dancing filled the streets, and even the secular bus drivers would wear costumes when doing their stops. It is a holiday of festive eating, parties, gift-giving of food baskets, charity giving, dressing up, music, dancing, plays, and of course drinking. The holiday that everyone would characterize as happy, uplifting, festive, and above all else, *fun*. And who doesn't want a fun holiday?

And yes, it is true, Purim is most certainly a fun holiday. But of course, like all of the Jewish holidays, there is so much more to it than meets the eye. Purim is, in some ways, the deepest of them all. In fact, there is a well-known statement in the Talmud that Yom Kippurim means literally a day "like" Purim, meaning that in some respects Purim is on a higher spiritual plane than even Yom Kippur. How are we to understand this? Yom Kippur, as we know, is a day when we reach spiritual heights unbeknownst to man. A day of no eating, no drinking, just immersing ourselves in prayer. A day when we are likened to the angels, as the liturgy even says. We even dress in white to wear the attire, so to speak, of the angels in Heaven. How can a day like Purim be compared to such a day? Yes, it is a day of commemorating a great miracle, and certainly the festivities are to help bring us to a greater awareness of what occurred on that day. But can it really be in the same league as Yom Kippur? And in some ways even *greater* than Yom Kippur?

So here begins the real secret of what Purim is all about. Before even taking a deeper look at the story, we can glean a lot just from the name of the holiday itself. Many of us may know that the word "Purim" comes from the word "*Pur*" which means a lottery. This term comes from the lottery that Haman used when he was trying to determine which day to annihilate the Jews. Couldn't there be a more inspiring name for this Holiday?

The answer lies in remembering what this Holiday represents, as well as remembering what our enemy in the Purim story represents. Haman came from the ancient tribe of Amalek, the sworn enemy of the Jewish People from Biblical times. Amalek is the only people we are commanded in the Torah to destroy completely, even women and children. There is an additional commandment to remember that which Amalek did to us, and we are commanded to read the verses concerning Amalek just before Purim. This is the only nation that we are required to remember that which they did to us. How are we to understand this? Can the character of one nation really be so evil that the Torah goes out of its way to single them out for annihilation? And why is it so important to remember that which Amalek did to us, right before Purim? Is there a deeper connection between the Purim story and Amalek, besides just the fact that Haman came from the tribe of Amalek. Examining the verses dealing with Amalek helps us to understand the character of this formidable foe. When in the Torah did we first encounter Amalek?

The answer is we find our first encounter with Amalek shortly after the splitting of the sea. The verses write that Amalek attacked us "Asher Korcha Baderech," "*When they happened to meet you* on the way." What was the significance of this phrase? Many of the commentators jump on it. They find alluded to in these words that Amalek preferred to attack us in a happenstance way, and in fact, their whole philosophy of life is "everything is happenstance." There is in all likelihood, no God, and if there is, he is no longer involved in human affairs. The classic "Clockwork theory" of the Universe; that God created this world, like one would wind back a clock, but then leftthe scene as the clock continues to do its work on its own.

Did their philosophy make an impression on the Jewish People? Unfortunately, for some Jews, it did. *Rashi,* the great medieval commentator points out that the word "Korcha" from the verse above can also mean "cold." He explains that Amalek succeeded, to a certain extent, in making us "cold," meaning less inspired, more distant spiritually. He likens it to someone who is jumps into scalding hot bath. Even though the person gets burned, he makes the water colder for others to now jump in. Amalek, so to speak, made the water cold. They placed doubts in our minds about God, about our own abilities, and about Divine Intervention. They also now made it easier for other nations which were afraid of our God to no longer be afraid.

We find this idea of Amalek elsewhere in the Torah as well. In another battle with Amalek, it is written that when Moses raised his arms, the Jews were victorious, and when he lowered them, Amalek was victorious. How are we to understand this? Was God's intervention really based on how long Moses could keep his arms up? Perhaps, there is a deeper meaning to the simple text. Moses, as we know, represented the Jewish People as their leader, when his hands were *metaphorically raised,* meaning when he felt all, is dependent upon our Father in Heaven, the Jewish People were able to be victorious. But then there were moments when his faith waned, when his hands *metaphorically felt heavy and were pulled to the ground,* meaning when he felt more reliant on the *ground* (earthly, natural forces), indeed they began to lose. For at those moments Amalek was, on a deeper level, winning, their ideology of Godlessness was winning, which in turn caused them to win on the battlefield as well.

And so we see why Amalek must be so utterly eradicated; their philosophy is the very antithesis of what Judaism is all about. Judaism is all about seeing Godliness around us, seeing God's Hidden Hand in all that we do, on a personal, national, and global level. Although nowadays we don't know who Amalek is, according to many commentaries, any nation or group of people which take on the Amalek ideology, is today's modern day Amalek. Many modern day sages believe Nazi Germany was modern day Amalek, as Hitler himself once stated in Mein Kampf "The Jews have brought two ills to the world, circumcision to the body and conscience to the soul." Indeed, much of the Nazis whole agenda was not only to rid the world of Jews, but to rid the world of Jewish articles as well, objects which bring Godliness into the world.

We see the agenda of Amalek in a different place as well, this time directly related to Haman himself. The Talmud asks "Where do we see Haman in the Torah?" The Talmud answers that we see it in the verses at the beginning of Genesis concerning Adam and Eve eating from the Tree of Knowledge of Good and Evil. The verse writes *"Hamin ha-etz asher tochlu"* which means *"From this* Tree you have eaten." The Talmud sees as a play on words *"Hamin"* as a hint to Haman. The question is, what possible connection is there between Haman and eating from the Tree of Knowledge of Good and Evil?

Rabbi Akiva Tatz answers the question beautifully. The Midrash and Talmud say that before Adam ate from the Tree, he did not have an internal Evil Inclination, he only had an external one. But internally, he *only had a knowledge of Goodness.* What does this mean? Rabbi Tatz gives a beautiful analogy. He says that when the Evil Inclination was external to Adam it was like standing at the edge of a cliff during daylight. Technically speaking, a person has free will about whether or not he or she wants to jump, but the consequences of the action are so clear to the person, that he or she would never do it. Once Adam ate from the Tree, and the Evil inclination became *internal* to him, it is like the same person standing at the edge of the cliff, only this time at nighttime. Now one cannot see what is beyond the edge of the cliff, he or she is no longer sure if it is only a few feet down, or if it is hundreds of feet down. (Why Adam and Eve chose to eat from the Tree is a discussion beyond the focus of this chapter.) This is why it was called the Tree of Knowledge of Good *and* Evil. Now both were a part of Adam's intrinsic nature. One becomes unsure of the consequences of one's actions. In short, one becomes doubtful of what is good and what is evil, and whether there is a God in the world who is watching and cares about our actions. This is the erosion of Faith, and this is what Haman and Amalek represented. This is the deeper connection between Haman and the Tree. Amalek, above all else brought *confusion* into the world, God's Presence as well as conscience is no longer felt as strongly anymore.

With this new understanding, the time has come now to examine some of the laws and customs surrounding the holiday of Purim. One of the most well-known customs on Purim is to dress up with masks and costumes. This seemingly superficial "fun" custom is actually laden with deeper meaning. On Purim we remember that in the world, nothing is as it seems. All of the superficiality of the world, the world of Amalek is not the real world, the real world is that which is underneath. In fact, the words *Megillas Esther*, which literally means "The Scroll of Esther" can have another meaning as well. Megillah can also mean *Megaleh* which means "To Reveal" and "Esther" can come from the word "Haster" which means "Hidden." Thus the words Megillas Esther can mean "To reveal that which is hidden!" An extraordinary idea indeed.

In fact, many of the main characters in the Esther story wear masks, sometimes not really identifying who they really are, or what their true motives are. Haman pretends to have the only the king's best interests in mind when he advises the king to annihilate the Jewish People, pretending that the Jews are a threat to his kingdom since they follow their own laws and customs, and not those of the rest of Persia. In reality he sought to destroy the Jews for his own evil genocidal wishes. Mordechai never reveals that he is a relative and friend of Esther's, it is Esther who reveals it to the king at the end. And of course, Esther herself wears a mask, she never reveals her true identity and intentions untilthe very end of the Esther story.

But of course there is one more who wears a mask throughout the story, and this is none other than God Himself. God's name is never mentioned once in the Megillah. In fact, the entire Purim story seems to come about completely through natural occurrences as there are no open miracles in the story. The Talmud alludes to this idea as well.

The Talmud asks, "Where do we find a hint to Esther from the Torah? From the verse, *"Anochi Aster, haster mipani"* which means "Behold I will hide My Face from you." The word Aster is a play on words and can hint to the name "Esther" which as we said above can mean "Hidden." Indeed, God is "Hidden" throughout the story and it is up to us to see His Hand. This is the beautiful irony. Amalek, as manifested through Haman in our story is trying to deny the Hand of God in everything, and right in this same story, God is telling us that although He appears to be Hidden, in fact he is orchestrating the whole story! When we are reading the story and celebrating Purim, we are being *Megalleh Esther*, we are "Revealing that which is hidden."

This also can explain an enigmatic passage in the Talmud. The Talmud in one place says that the Jewish People reached a higher spiritual level at the time of the redemption in the Purim story than at the Revelation at Mount Sinai. How are we to understand this? Mount Sinai was the greatest revelation ever given to Man in history! How can the Purim story possibly be greater than that? But herein lies the answer; for the revelation was *just that, it was an open manifestation of God in the world, but Purim was revealing God in the world even in natural occurrences.* When the Jewish People were able to destroy Haman not only physically, but ideologically at the end of the Purim story and reaffirm God's Hand in everything, even in the course of nature, that, indeed was a greater spiritual level.

I believe the Purim story has taught us that the task today is to see God behind the headlines, so to speak, to see His hand not only in our everyday lives, but also in world events. One such recent example of this was The Gulf War of the early 1990s. Many may recall the headlines, but few could appreciate the miraculous nature of some of the events. Saddam Hussein launched 39 SCUD missiles to densely populated areas in Israel. Given the size of these missiles and the fact that there are over 500 pounds of explosives in each of them, this should have caused thousands of casualties, but actually only led to one direct hit that resulted in a death. One story was that a SCUD missile directly hit a bomb shelter in Tel Aviv that was also made into a makeshift synagogue. At the time, the bomb shelter was loaded to the brim with 200 people. The entire bomb shelter was destroyed except ironically the one wall which housed the Ark (where the Torah scroll is kept). All of the people at the time were near the ark praying. Of the 200 people there, there was not one reported injury. Incredibly, the Gulf War, which many predicted would last for many more months and maybe even years, ended on Purim day. The story gets even more bizarre when archeological evidence points to the fact that ancient Persia of the Purim story is today modern day Iraq, where The Gulf War took place. And Saddam, much like Haman, declared his hope to one day destroy Israel and all of the Jewish People. One can look at the parallels in the story and dismiss them all as mere coincidences and "good luck" or one can see God's Hidden Hand even in these modern day events.

With this new understanding of some of the deeper meanings in the Purim story, we can also explain one of the more well-known, but mystifying laws of drinking wine at the Purim *Seudah* (Purim festive meal). Judaism in general is not a religion of indulgences, its laws generally require a certain amount of discipline. However, suddenly in regard to the Purim *Seudah*, we are encouraged to drink, and according to many *Poskim* (deciders of Jewish Law) even drink to the point of intoxication! How are we to understand this?

We all know too well what often occurs when a person becomes inebriated with alcohol. All inhibitions are lost. Often, we see "the real person" sometimes for all its glory, sometimes for all its ugliness. The Talmud notes that the Hebrew word for "wine" is *"yayin"* which in Gematria (numerical value) equals 70, the same numerical value as the word "sod" which means "secret." The Talmud writes *"Nichanas Yayin, Yazah Sod,"* meaning "Wine comes in, secrets come out." Here we see a hint to what we have been speaking about; namely that Purim is all about remembering that we often wear masks, and that this is not reality. On Purim we wear masks, but it is to help us remember who we really are, and that often what appears to be on the surface isn't reality at all. The wine can help us finally be "real." It can help bring out an inner yearning to look at the world in a different way, perhaps with a more spiritual lens. Wine, only when taken in its proper time, can help us to see a higher spiritual reality.

Perhaps it is for these reasons that the Talmud says that the Story of Esther is like *"Ayelet Hashachar,"* the "first rays of dawn" which appear right when the night ends. The Talmud says this is like Esther, which is the end of all miracles. What does this mean? On a simple level, it means this is the last recorded miracle of the Bible, for shortly after this the Bible canon was closed. However, on a deeper level, I believe this passage in the Talmud is alluding to what we are speaking about here. The darkest part of the night is at the very end, just before dawn, for it is the moments that the stars, the moon, and the constellations in the sky are no longer shining. It is precisely at this moment that the rays of dawn begin to break through the horizon. So too with the Esther story. It is specifically at the *darkest of times,* when the metaphysical night is at its very end, when we are able to see God's light shining through. The last of all miracles, the Talmud is teaching us, is done in this way. The Talmud was conveying that the world is transitioning to a more "natural" state, where the "supernatural miracle" will cease to exist. It is up to us to see the miracles within nature. In this way, Purim isn't only the end of miracles of the Bible, in some ways, it is the *greatest* of all the miracles of the Bible, for it prepares us best for the world which we now live in.

With these new understandings, we can now answer our original question regarding how in some ways Purim can place us at an even higher spiritual level than Yom Kippur. Yom Kippur is a day of total withdrawal, Purim is *inviting* indulgences, but using them for a higher Purpose! Purim becomes the very antithesis of what Amalek is. It is saying that even with all of the confusion, all of the physical pleasure that exist in the world, one can *still see God in them*, still be able to utilize this world to bring ourselves closer to God. Amalek says the pleasures we see around us is all that there is, Judaism teaches us these pleasures are so much more than just that. Who is on a higher spiritual level, the ascetic monk who meditates on the mountaintop, or the person who very much lives in this world, but rises above it? Judaism teaches us it is the latter. It isn't only about ascending to Heaven, it is about bringing the world around him together with him. In this way, in a very real and tangible way, we are defeating Amalek each year; we are remembering what it means to be a Jew and to live our lives on the deepest level we can.

The Power of Jewish Unity

There are three main laws concerning the Holiday of Purim in addition to the reading of the Megillah. These three are *Matonot LeEvyonim* (giving charity to the poor), *Mishloach Manot* (fruit gift baskets to friends), and *Seudat Purim* (the festive meal on Purim). What is significant about these three *Mitzvot*? Is there any correlation, or common theme of these three, to explain why they are singled out?

Perhaps an answer to this question is to look at some of the underlying causes of the near annihilation of the Jewish People as well as the causes for their salvation. One often overlooked aspect to the Purim story is the complete disunity of the Jewish People at the beginning of the story. Many Jews were assimilating very quickly into Persian culture. In fact, they were participating in Ahasureus's (Achashverosh's) feast at the beginning of the story. This undoubtedly had non-kosher food, as well as promiscuous activities, as evident from the story. Taking part in Persian culture drew a tremendous rift amongst other Jews, who saw this as a slippery slope in Jewish values. However, at the end of the story, we find that the Jewish People were very much unified both in prayer and fasting. In fact, according to the Midrash, Mordechai organized a night of learning Torah to be done by children everywhere to help annul the degree of annihilation. This Night, the Midrash says, was very significant, since it turned out to be the night that the King couldn't sleep, and he discovered the good deed Mordechai did. That night ended up being the beginning of the redemption. Many commentators say that the "King" referred to here, wasn't Achashverosh, but the Master of the World, Himself. He, so to speak, "couldn't sleep" because He saw the unity of the Jewish People, that even all of the children were participating in a night of Torah study. So the salvation was only able to come about when the Jewish people were unified.

Now we can return to the three primary laws for this unique Holiday. All three of them center on Jewish unity. Giving money to the poor certainly brings a sense of unity. Giving fruit baskets to our friends also brings about unity, especially since the actual law is that the basket shouldn't only be given to our friends, but to our enemies as well. And certainly a festive Purim Seudah (meal), where one inevitably invites friends and family, brings about a sense of unity as well.

Sadly, all too often, it is tragedy or crisis that brings Jews together. We experienced this recently when three boys were kidnapped in Israel, and this brought an unprecedented level of prayer from Jews of all walks of life all over the world. Although, sadly enough, it was discovered that these three boys were murdered, it led to a confrontation with Hamas and the discovery of terror tunnels that were about to be used to murder and kidnap Jews in Southern Israel on a very massive level. And so a potential massive terrorist attack had been averted. However, we should not wait for a crisis to strike to bring Jews together. The message of the Purim story should serve as a constant reminder to put aside our differences and unite, whether in good times or difficult times. The power of unity can bring the Jewish People to extraordinary heights that we would not otherwise be able to achieve.

A Modern-Day Purim Story

There has been much talk in recent years of the so-called "Bible Code," that is, of finding hidden words through numerical sequencing in the Torah that allude to future historical events and personalities. By nature, I am very skeptical of such "codes" as I believe, as many have proven, that such "codes" can be found in any book, if one were to try every type of numerical sequencing out there. What further aggravates proving any validity to such "codes" is why only certain words regarding an event are found in the Torah, whereas other words are not. For example, in the "code" regarding the Gulf War, the code may find "Schwarzkopf" the famous US General at the time, but not "Colin Powell," the equally important military chief at the time. So why only some words appear in code, but others do not, makes the validity of such "codes" suspect. As such, I believe, with good reason, these "codes" are often relegated to covers of tabloid magazines, which are known for fantastical, often completely untrue, headlines.

However, with this being said, there is one code that I believe stands head and shoulders above all other codes, one that I have found to be so remarkable that it is nearly impossible to dismiss as mere coincidence or fabrication. This code is well known in most orthodox circles, but is virtually unknown to the rest of the Jewish world, let alone, the world at large. This code is definitely worthy of mention, and even for those who already know it, it is worth repeating for the sole purpose of strengthening ones faith in the veracity of the Torah as a Divine document.

The Book of Esther, according to Jewish tradition, was written by Queen Esther herself, who according to the Talmud, was a prophetess. As a prophetess, she would be able to at times "see" future events, based on divinely given intuition.

Let us turn to one passage in the Book of Esther. At the end of the Purim story, the Book lists the ten sons of Haman who were also hung, besides Haman himself. When listing the ten sons, there were three letters that were written in smaller letters than the rest of the letters. These Hebrew letters are "Tuf" "Shin" and "Zayin." No one ever knew why these letters were smaller than the others, but because we have a Jewish tradition that the Torah must be preserved exactly as it is, every copy of the Torah for thousands of years always has these three letters smaller than the rest. What do those three letters mean? Those three letters spell the Hebrew date for the year 1946.

What event occurred in 1946? The Nuremburg trials, in which ten Nazis were hung, exactly the same fate of hanging that the ten sons of Haman had. Bizarre coincide? Perhaps so.

But here is where the story gets even more remarkable, to the point where even the greatest of skeptics will admit that they are indeed baffled. The last of the ten Nazis, Julius Streicher, as he mounted the gallows, suddenly blurted out "Purim Fest 1946." Those were the last words he said, and it is well documented in *Newsweek Magazine* and numerous other journals and historical records.

What was he thinking when he screamed out those words? What connection did he suddenly make to the Purim Holiday? He was not hung on Purim day. And why specifically did he mention the year 1946? It is highly improbable that he just blurted out those words randomly, without any significance, as he knew he was the very last Nazi to be hung, and his words would be recorded for posterity. Again, I turn to the skeptics who are reading these words, *what was he thinking when he blurted out those words? And why were those three specific letters, and only those letters, always written smaller? Why was the year 1946 mentioned in a document written thousands of years ago?*

I am normally not one who is big into "proving" that the Torah is Divine, I believe much of the Torah's authorship is, if anything, very difficult to prove. God, I believe, purposely made it difficult to prove, to help us maintain a level of free will and to choose on our own to still have Faith in Him and His Word. However, I also believe that God occasionally in the Torah gave us "road marks," little hints in His Book to remind us that yes, indeed, it all comes from Him. It is up to us to find these "hidden marks" to help us remember on our journey that the Good Book is His, and He is with us every step of the way. He is here with us today, just as much as He was there with us thousands of years ago when the Biblical stories occurred.

Spiritual Exercises

1. In the month of Adar, the month when Purim occurs, there is a special Mitzvah to be joyful. Try to think of ways during this month to make your life more joyful. Even simple things like watching comedy acts online or listening to upbeat music can help with this. My favorite way is to simply spend a little more time with my children, count my blessings, and appreciate the joy that they have brought to my life.

2. Spend some time during Adar leading up to Purim studying the Book of Esther. By studying, I mean not only reading through the story, but through the magnificent commentaries as well. This not only brings the story more to life but will offer insights into the story that you may not otherwise see.

3. Try to make the day of Purim itself special. If possible, take off from work that day. Try to attend a live music event that night which has dancing as well. Watch funny Purim videos online to help put you in the mood of being happy that day and feeling the Holiday more.

4. Spend time on Purim fulfilling the commandments of the day. These are giving fruit/candy baskets to friends, giving money to the poor, hearing the Megillah being read, and having a Purim *Seudah* (festive meal.)

5. Make these commandments as meaningful as possible. Perhaps give a fruit basket to someone who you didn't get along with so well, to make amends. Try to think of an organization that really helps the poor a lot, or individuals who really need the money. And during the *Seudah*, drink some wine, and try to get not only a physical high, but a spiritual high as well. Use it as an opportunity to connect to God and the Jewish People.

Passover:
A New Journey as Old As Time

"And this (God's blessings and the Torah) is what kept our fathers and what keeps us surviving. For, not only one arose and tried to destroy us, rather in every generation they try to destroy us, and God saves us from their hands."

-Passover Seder Liturgy

T HE STORY OF PASSOVER IS the cornerstone of the Jewish Faith. No words are repeated more often in the Bible than the words "Remember that which I did for your ancestors in Egypt." Indeed, Passover is perhaps the most well-known of all the Jewish Holidays and certainly the most celebrated. Indeed, no story has garnered as much attention as this ancient Biblical story. The story is retold by countless number of Jews and even non-Jews each year. Every year families gather around the table, often three generations or more, children, parents, grandparents, and perhaps great-grandparents to share the story of our extraordinary beginnings of the birth of our Nation in the oldest of all our Holidays. Indeed, while the Abraham story may be the birth of our *People*, the Exodus story is our birth as a *Nation*. It is not only the story of slavery to freedom, it is the story of despair to redemption, of poverty to riches, of chaos to unity, and above all, faithlessness to faithfulness. It is, indeed, the greatest story ever told.

The entire Torah is called a *Sefer Torah*, where the word *Sefer* is commonly translated as a "scroll" of Torah. However, the word *Sefer* can also mean *Sipur* which means to tell over, usually referring to a story. Indeed, the entire Torah is, to a certain extent a story that we are meant to tell over to our children. In the *Shema* prayer, that is said daily and is regarded as one of the most important prayers we say, it contains the words from the Torah *Veshinantam Levanecha* which means you shall teach your children. The Torah goes on to say the imperative to teach our sons wherever we are, whether we are in the comforts of our own home or travelling on the way, whether it is in the morning or at night. Passing on these stories is known as the *Mesorah*, or Tradition, and it is the bedrock of the Jewish Faith.

Although there is great emphasis on teaching the Torah to our children, there is an even greater emphasis on this when it comes to sharing the story of the Exodus. The phrase given numerous times throughout the Haggadah is *Sipur Yitziat Mitzraim*, which means "tell over the story of the Exodus." In one place in the Torah which the Talmud expounds on, it is written that we have a specific commandment to mention the Exodus every single day. We fulfill this commandment when we say the Shema, which we are commanded to say twice every day. So the Exodus is in many ways the highlight of our prayers as well.

There are so many themes of Passover, and it is perhaps the richest of all our traditions. One can fill volumes discussing this Holiday, and its countless aspects and perspectives. I will try, as best as I can, to fit this giant Holiday into one short chapter. To do this, I will only focus on the main aspects of the Holiday, that is, to only discuss the forest, and not the trees.

The focal point of Passover is of course the Seder. The word "Seder" means "Order" since indeed it is an order of ascension throughout the night. The Seder consists of 15 steps, which symbolizes the 15 steps to enter the ancient Temple as well as the fifteen "Songs of Ascension" written by King David in the Book of Psalms. This again is hinting to the idea that there is an order of ascension toward holiness. The Seder is, above all, a build-up toward a finale. It is also by no coincidence that the famous "*Dayenu*" song which we sing in the Haggadah also consists of 15 stanzas, for it is an order of ascension from leaving Egypt, through receiving the Torah, and finally coming to the Land of Israel.

This explains why the Haggadah seems to switch from discussing our slavery to soon transitioning into our freedom, for this is the order of our ascension. I believe even the *Mah Nishtana*, the famous Four Questions hint to this idea. The first two of the four questions seem to deal with slavery. It asks about eating Maror, the bitter herb which is of course the great symbolism of the bitterness of our slavery. The second question is about eating Matzah, which is called *"Lechem Oni"* the "Poor Man's Bread" which again symbolizes slavery and hardship. Then we switch into questions about our freedom in the final two questions. We ask about our dipping, and only wealthy people are accustomed to having dips for food as poor people cannot afford them. And we ask about our reclining in our chairs, once again a symbol of wealth and freedom.

But there is more that the Haggadah is trying to convey by beginning with slavery and ending with freedom. It is more than just an order of ascension. Although the central theme is telling over the story of the Exodus, Seder night is much more than just a retelling, if you will. It is in many ways a re-enactment, and in some ways, even a re-experiencing. So many of the laws and rituals which surround the Seder night are concerned with acting at first as though we are slaves and then later in the Haggadah we act as free people. There is one passage in the Haggadah where we see this the most succinctly. But before we examine this passage, we must review a Talmudic law that *before* performing a commandment in the Torah we say a blessing on the commandment we are about to perform. There is only one well-known exception and that is for a person who is converting to Judaism. The final part of the conversion process involves immersing in the *Mikvah*, or ritual bath. Normally a blessing is said before going into the *Mikvah*, however, a convert only says this blessing *after* he or she immersed in the *Mikvah*. This change in the normal procedure is for the simple reason that the person has not yet entered into the Jewish covenant and therefore cannot yet fulfill the *Mitzvah* of saying a blessing. A convert only says the blessing *after* they have gone to the *Mikvah* and become part of the Jewish People.

There is one other place that Jewish law seems to make this same exception, and that is on Passover night. Although we are obligated on Passover night to say a blessing on the Mitzvah of telling over the story of the Exodus, instead of saying the blessing at the *beginning* of *Maggid*, (which is the portion that discusses the story of the Exodus) we say it at the *end*! Why do we say the blessing at the end? Once again, it is this same idea; at the beginning of Maggid we are literally like slaves who are not obligated in Mitzvot, and therefore certainly not obligated to say the blessing on the Mitzvot. However, by the end of *Maggid* we become free people, and so the obligation to say the blessing is upon us. What a powerful idea, where our journey through the Exodus story actually effects Jewish Law as well!

So we begin the Seder night talking about not only how we were once not only slaves in Egypt, but idol-worshippers as well. In fact, the beginning passage is said in Aramaic, not in the Holy Tongue of Hebrew. Why is it so important to remember our beginnings? Since only through remembering our beginnings can we come to fully appreciate where we are now. People who rise to greatness only retain their greatness when they remember their humble beginnings. Otherwise, haughtiness sets in. We even make a declaration at the beginning of the Seder; we make an open invitation for anyone who wants to, may come and join us. This is more of a declaration to ourselves, to understand and appreciate our freedom and use it as a vehicle to reach out to others. A slave does not have the ability to give voluntarily; he is forced to give to his master. One of the greatest expressions of freedom is to *choose* to give to others. Through this we show not only our appreciation of freedom, but that we can utilize freedom in the greatest ways possible. It is through this declaration to invite the needy as guests to our Seder table that we are acknowledging and expressing our gratitude for our freedom.

The Jewish people are in fact, known for their ability to express gratitude to the One Above for their triumphs and blessings. In fact, the Jewish People are even called in Hebrew *Yehudim* which comes from the word *Hodah,* which means gratitude. And so we begin the story of the Exodus by inviting everyone to come who may not have a meal, for we remember that we too were once hungry for food. And we end the story of the Exodus, at the end of Maggid with the blessing "Blessed are You God, the Redeemer of Israel." This blessing again affirms our thankfulness to God for the kindness He has done to us in Egypt.

There is a beautiful insight from the *Lubavitcher Rebbe* which expands on this Pesach theme of slavery to Redemption as well. We know that the culmination of the Ten Plagues was the final plague, that is, the plague of the First Born. In fact, the name "Passover" is based on the idea that God "passed over" so to speak the Jewish homes that had markings on their doors when He brought down the tenth plague. So obviously, the tenth plague was of extreme significance. The *Rebbe* points out that this was the only plague of which God said precisely when it would occur in the Torah, namely at Midnight. Why was it significant to tell us when the plague would occur, and why specifically at midnight? In order to understand the Rebbe's answer to these questions, it is important to understand that the Jewish midnight isn't at 12:00 AM the way the secular day is divided, rather it is literally *halfway* through the night, that is halfway between sunrise and sunset. This is a time that would fluctuate throughout the year, depending on how long the night is. So true midnight is that moment of transition, when the very darkest point of the night begins to turn to light. This is what God was teaching us with the tenth plague, this was that cathartic moment when Oppression would end, and Redemption would begin. This is what we are celebrating on Pesach, and this is why the symbolism of both slavery and freedom are so rich that night, for we are celebrating that transition. This transition often takes place in a single moment. But what a difference a moment can make! From Darkness into Light, indeed.

It is interesting to note that the word *Matzah*, the unleavened bread which we are required to eat on Passover, is very similar in Hebrew letters to the word *Chametz,* which is the leavened bread that we are forbidden to eat on Passover. In fact, if one was to lay out the 3 Hebrew letters of these two words, there would only be a very small line which differentiates between these two. This surely can be no coincidence. Why would these two words which have such opposite meanings, be spelled with almost identical letters? The commentators explain this beautifully with this idea we have just shared. *Chametz* represents laziness, while *Matzah* represents zeal and alacrity. Often the difference between slavery and freedom is just a split moment. When we are inspired in life, even for a split moment, it is that moment that we must act. For if we wait, if we delay, then our own self-doubts and haughtiness often creep in, and our opportunity is lost forever. How often does a special Mitzvah come our way and we wait a moment too long and the opportunity is gone forever? Often one simple good deed can have very dramatic repercussions which we may not ever be aware of. *True* freedom is not just free will, it is the ability to overcome our base urges and voluntarily *choose* the right path. *Carpi Diem*, Seize the Day, as the expression goes. This is the message of Passover, and the message of the Matzah. Act with zeal, as the Jewish People did on Passover night. Do not wait, for then the moment is lost forever.

Redeeming Ourselves

One of the great mystical numbers we see on Seder night is the number four. Four cups of wine, four questions at the Seder, the Four Sons, and four expressions of Redemption. Let us now explore one of these four.

The one which has always puzzled me the most was the Four Sons. Just to do a quick review, we suddenly pause the Haggadah narrative to mention that the Torah seems to speak of four sons, and phrases how they would relate to the story of the Exodus. These "four sons" are the wise son, the wicked son, the simpleton, and the one who is afraid to ask. Why in the middle of the Haggadah do we suddenly talk about four sons, and how they would discuss the story of the Exodus? What relevance do these hypothetical sons have to us and to the story of the Exodus?

I believe the answer has very much to do with what we are try to accomplish by retelling the story of the Exodus. Many people believe that we are merely try to pass on the *Mesorah* or tradition, to the next generation for what happened to us in Egypt at the time of the Exodus. However, I believe it is much deeper than this. The answer is hinted to in the laws of a different passage in the Haggadah, namely, the *Mah Nishtana*. The *Mah Nishtana*, perhaps the most well-known portion in the Haggadah asks four questions concerning why the night of Passover is different from all other nights.

We all know of the well-known custom of *Ma Nishtana*, which is to have our children read The Four Questions. However, according to Jewish Law, if one doesn't have children or a spouse and is eating the

Seder alone, one must ask the questions out loud to oneself. How are we to understand this? What can one possibly gain by asking the questions to oneself? It is one thing if children are present, as we want to arouse their curiosity, but it is another thing entirely to ask the questions when one already knows the answers!

The answer is that although it is imperative to teach our children the story of the Exodus and the origins of our People, ultimately the most important aspect of the Seder is still to teach it to ourselves. By teaching it to others we are helping to reinforce it for ourselves, but ultimately it is *ourselves* that are the most important when it comes to the story. In fact, the Seder says in each generation we are obligated to feel as if *we* were the ones who left Egypt. So the story of the Exodus isn't really about what took place long ago and it isn't even about what we teach our children. It is about *us*. What freedom means to *us*. What it means to *us* to be a part of the Jewish People. This is what Pesach is all about, and this is how we grow spiritually from this extraordinary holiday.

So now we can return to the Four Sons. I believe these Four Sons represent the struggle within all of us. It is very much our story. There are moments in our lives when we are indeed like the Wise Son, always thirsty for spiritual knowledge, and to have a greater understanding of Judaism. And then there are times when we feel simple, when we just want to have a simple Faith and no need to understand it all. Then there are times when we are plagued with questions, questions of Faith, but are afraid to ask, afraid of what we may find. And finally, there are times when we feel no sense of faith at all, when we don't feel like we want to have anything to do with our tradition at all, much like the Wicked Son. The lesson of the Four Sons is that still despite our struggles, our highs and lows, we still come to the Seder. We take our frailties with us, and still come to recount the Exodus story. This is a parallel connection to what we studied earlier regarding the Four Species in the Sukkot chapter, where we take the many struggles within us and still bind them together and come to serve God.

Another passage in the Maggid section of the Haggadah that has always captured my imagination is the story of the five great sages sitting together in the city of Bnai Brak. The story tells that they spent the entire night discussing the story of the Exodus, until one of their students came and told them that dawn had come and so the time to say *Kriat Shema* (the Shema Prayer) had arrived. I was always fascinated by this story since I feel there is more to it than meets the eye; and that is what made it deserving of being included in the Haggadah. How so? I believe there is a great deal of symbolism here. Discussing it at *night* I believe is symbolic of our long and bitter exile, which is always compared to night in Talmudic and Midrashic literature. Moreover, the story's emphasis on discussing the great miracles of the Exodus is to help remind us and inspire us during this long and bitter exile that God is still with us today just as he was in the days of the Exodus. Finally, the symbolism of dawn arriving, the great symbol of the Messianic age, when we all declare the words of the Shema, which speak of God's Oneness, and His concern for our daily lives, is fitting. The Messianic age will be the ultimate expression of "loving the Lord our God with all of our hearts and souls" as the Shema declares.

The Song of All Songs

During the Holiday of Passover, we read one of the most profound and inspiring, but often misunderstood portions in the entire Torah. This portion is called *Shir Hashirim* translated as Song of Songs, and was written by none other than King Solomon himself. The portion on a simple textual level, which is certainly beautiful itself, discusses the passionate love a man and wife have for each other. However, nearly all the commentaries, and most notably *Rashi*, explain it as an allegorical love between God and the Jewish People. It is then perhaps no wonder that the great Talmudic sage Rabbi Akiva said that although all of the writings of the Prophets are holy, *Shir Hashirim* is the holy of holies. It is perhaps this allegorical understanding that makes the work so profound, and why we read this portion specifically on Passover. For although all the other Holidays also focus on our relationship with God (Shavuot especially, when we received the Divine Book for how to bring ourselves closer to Him), it is only on Passover that we *began* our relationship with Him. While Abraham, the first Jew, began his relationship with God centuries before, it is only on Passover that we began collectively as a People to develop a relationship with Him. Perhaps this is why we read this Book on Passover. Every loving couple always will fondly talk about the day they first met, and how their relationship evolved from then. For all is contained in the beginning.

The Song of the Sea

On the final day of Passover, according to Jewish tradition, was the day of the Splitting of the Sea. In Israel, this day is celebrated for one day, but in the Diaspora, because of ancient calendar reasons, it is celebrated as two days. The Splitting of the Sea is one of the pinnacles of Jewish history. Indeed, if you were to ask any Jew which moment in the Bible they wish they could be there for, most people would invariably answer the Splitting of the Sea. Indeed, the Splitting of the Sea has captured the imagination of countless numbers of artists over the years. The Midrash writes that at the Splitting of the Sea even a simple maidservant reached a higher spiritual level than when Ezekiel received his greatest prophetic vision *Maasah Merkavah* (The Parable of the Chariot). In fact, the only time in the Torah where the entire Jewish People burst into song was at the splitting of the sea (there were other places of song in the Torah, but they were typically by one individual such as Moses or King David.) To illustrate just how paramount to our faith the splitting of the sea was, each day in our morning prayers, we recite the *Az Yashir,* the entire song which the Jewish People sang after the sea split.

What was so unique about the splitting of the sea that it is elevated to such a status not only at the time it occurred, but even today? I believe the answer is twofold. For one, the splitting of the sea represented a watershed in Jewish history in that it was, above all else, a point of no return. When the plagues were raining down on Egypt, while it may have encouraged the Egyptians to free the Jewish People, the Jews *were still in Egypt* when this occurred. The idea that we were one day to become a separate and independent people was still foreign to them. When the splitting of the sea occurred, the transition into an independent nation became final. Now there was literally a sea separating us from Egypt. There was no turning back, our redemption from slavery had become complete. And so it was time to sing.

However, I believe there was an even more powerful message behind the splitting of the sea, one which still resonates to us this very day. The Splitting of the Sea represents a clear demonstration of God's mastery over nature in a way that even the ten plagues did not. While the ten plagues were certainly miraculous, they didn't necessarily stop at a crucial moment, rather they each just faded, but there was no significance in when they stopped. However, regarding the Splitting of the Sea, the sea miraculously returned to its original position *just as the Egyptian army entered it.* This was a blatant display of God's total control over Nature, that He in fact *created* Nature, and it is up to Him to bend it at will, and then restore Nature to its regular state. In fact, the Midrash even writes that built into the blueprint so to speak of the creation of the Red Sea was that it was created on the condition it would split at the correct moment and return to its normal state at the correct moment.

I wrote in my first book "The Hidden Path" a beautiful parable from the *Klosenberger Rebbe* about the Splitting of the Sea that is worth repeating here. The parable is about a sculptor who wanted to sculpt his greatest masterpiece. He decided to sculpt a horse. He spent a long time closely studying the anatomy and colors of a horse before beginning the slow process of sculpting and painting the horse. When the project was completed, the horse looked magnificent, and he proudly brought it to the middle of the marketplace for all to see. To his shock and disappointment, no one paid any attention to it. Why? Because they thought it was a real horse and no one pays attention to just a regular horse! So what did he do? *He split the horse in half!* And *now*, when everyone passed the horse, they said "Wow, now that's a horse!" The parable is so simple and yet so profound and beautiful. We can all appreciate the extraordinary miracle of the Splitting of the Sea, but the real miracle is the sea itself! Sometimes it takes a miracle to appreciate what was already there.

This, I believe is the *madrega* (spiritual level) that the Jewish people reached at the time of the Splitting of the sea. They were able to see the entire symphony of creation and nature, both miraculous and non-miraculous as orchestrated by the All-Encompassing God. And they were able to see God's total control over every aspect of the world we live in. All was created by Him, all is sustained by Him, and all can be manipulated at will by Him. It was this discovery that led the Jewish

People to sing. They had seen Him not only vanquish their enemies, but do it in the most glorious, wondrous and comprehensive manner possible.

This idea is even hinted to in the words of their song *Az Yashir*. It is written "In the greatness of your majesty you threw down those who opposed you. You unleashed your burning anger; it consumed them like stubble. By the blast of your nostrils the waters piled up. The surging waters stood up like a wall; the deep waters congealed in the heart of the sea. The enemy boasted, 'I will pursue, I will overtake them. I will divide the spoils; I will gorge myself on them. I will draw my sword and my hand will destroy them.' But you blew with your breath, and the sea covered them. They sank like lead in the mighty waters. Who among the gods is like you, Lord? Who is like you—majestic in holiness, awesome in glory, working wonders?" Within these words we see an understanding of God that there is none besides Him, and His power over our world is all-encompassing. It is therefore no wonder that the Splitting of the Sea and the subsequent song of *Az Yashir* has had such a lasting impact on the world, and that we are still feeling its reverberations to this very day. There is something calming in knowing what the Jewish People discovered back then; that God has total control over our world and we can always turn to Him, not only to listen to us, but to help us as well.

The end of the *Az Yashir* prayer is a prayer and a yearning for a future day, a prayer that the entire world will come to this greater understanding of God: "The saviors (of the Jewish People) will ascend Mount Zion to judge Esau's mountain (kingdom) and the kingdom will be God's. The God will be King over all the world, on that day God will be One, and His Name will be One." The Talmud teaches us the month of Nissan, which is the month of Passover is called the "*Zman Hageula*" that is, the Time of the Redemption, and that the ultimate redemption of the Messiah will come during this month. Indeed, there are customs inthis month which differentiate it from all other months of the Jewish calendar. Let us hope and pray for the Messiah to come very soon, when the world will come to this great realization.

A Passover Story

The story is told about the great Rabbi Levi Yitzchok of Berditchev. He went around his town on the eve of Passover looking for all the local smugglers. When he asked for contraband like tobacco, brocades, and embroideries he was able to get anything for the right price. However, when he asked the same smugglers for bread or whiskey they looked exasperated. They said to him "Rabbi, are you trying to insult us? The Seder will start in only a few hours and no Jew would have even a speck of *Chametz* left in his home or business." No matter what Rabbi Levi offered, he was not able to get any bread or liquor from them. The town had become completely chametz free.

Rabbi Levi seemed overjoyed to hear the smugglers' response. Rabbi Levi smiled radiantly and looked up to heaven and declared, "God almighty look down at the faithfulness of your People! Everyone knows the Czar has border guards and Tax Commissioners dedicated to his commands. The police and the courts are devoted to tracking down and punishing smugglers and black marketers and yet anything one could possibly want is still available. Now contrast this with the faith and Fidelity of Your children! it has been over 3000 years since you commanded us to observe Passover. No police, no guards, no courts and jails are in to enforce this edict and yet every Jew keeps your laws to the utmost. *Mi K'Amcha Yisruel,* who is like Your nation Israel?"

I have always liked this little vignette, for it illustrates the beauty of the Jewish People, keeping tradition as they have for thousands of years. Czars, police, and enforcers come and go, but Passover and its beautiful traditions and customs are here to stay.

Spiritual Exercises

1. Remember a time in your life when you thought deeply about the story of the Exodus. What drew you to the story?

2. What part of the story do you feel the most connected to? Why do you feel most connected to that part of the story?

3. How does thinking about the story of the Exodus make you feel? As a Jew? In your relationship with God?

4. Try to think of ways to incorporate the Exodus story more into your daily conscience. Perhaps begin by thinking a little more deeply, when saying the words that mention remembering the story of the Exodus in the Shema. Then monitor how this affects your Judaism.

The Modern-Day Jewish Holidays: God's Role in the Present Day

Introduction: Are these Holidays Necessary?

I WAS SOMEWHAT TORN WITH WRITING this chapter due to the controversy that it may stir, as well as the fact that it will almost certainly alienate some segments of the Orthodox Jewish community. These segments of the Jewish community I still lovingly embrace, although, admittedly, I differ somewhat regarding practical Jewish ideology. So, before I launch into some of the Torah insights, I find it imperative to delve deeply into the historical and religious significance of these Holidays.

Many in the Orthodox community reject these Holidays since we are no longer in Biblical times. They believe we are not allowed, per Jewish law, to celebrate or commemorate events based on modern day experiences. Even Chanukah, which occurred after the Biblical canon was closed, still occurred in the early days of the Talmud and when the 2nd Jewish Temple was still standing, as well as celebrating an open miracle.

However, I disagree with this assertion, since there are no *real* laws associated with these days, merely customs. As such, customs can be adopted at any point in Jewish history, as have occurred. Two examples that come to mind, are *Tashlich* and *Kaparot*, both of which began sometime in the Middle Ages. There is a small segment of the Orthodox Jewish community which says the customary *Hallel* with a blessing, which may render it to a more prominent level. However, this segment

103

of the Orthodox community is very much in the minority, and has its own Rabbinic authorities it relies on.

For now, let us focus on two of the modern day Holidays, namely Yom Haatzmaut and Yom Yerushalayim. Sadly enough, many Jews disregard the miraculous birth of the modern-day State of Israel as an insignificant event since it came about in a natural manner. However, nothing could be further from the truth. The story of Esther, where salvation occurred without a single open miracle, where God's name is not even mentioned once, teaches us that often the greatest of all miracles can come about in a natural manner. It is up to us to see the Hand of God in everything.

However, one of the greatest criticisms which are especially leveled against *Yom Haaztmaut* and *Yom Yerushalayim* are that salvations which come about through non-religious Jews, and sometimes even *anti*-religious Jews cannot have any spiritual or religious significance. However, I believe this to be incorrect. *Rabbi Ahron Soloveichik*, in his seminal work "Logic of the Heart, Logic of the Mind" grapples with this very same question.

He quotes a story from the Bible that proves that redemption can come through people that are irreligious. The story, which is in the Book of Kings, is about four lepers who were excommunicated and were forced to live outside of the Jewish camp. The leprosy we speak of here is a spiritual form of leprosy, and was the punishment in Biblical times for speaking words of *Loshon Harah*, damaging gossip about one's friend. The story occurred during a famine, when the Jews were on the verge of total starvation. These four Lepers decided to sneak into a tent of the Philistine army, which was encamped next door one night and steal some food as they too were famished. Lo and Behold! They discovered that during the night, the Philistine army fled, leaving behind all of their food! The Lepers could not believe their luck. They had only discovered this since they were outside of the Jewish camp and were thus able to sneak into the Philistine camp. The Lepers went back into the Jewish camp and informed the Jewish leaders that the Philistine army had fled, and the Jewish people were able to go to where the Philistines had encamped and partake of all the food they left behind. Thus, the famine ended, and the saviors were none other than these four lepers, who were sinners.

And so, it was with the modern-day State. Although many of the people who brought about the creation of the state were not religious people, and some were even anti-religious, nevertheless the spiritual benefits we have received as a people have been unparalleled in recent history. Now, for the first time in nearly 2000 years, Jews are free to go to the Land of Israel to visit, to study, to pray at the holy sites, and most importantly, to *live*.

I believe to a certain extent, that to not celebrate important dramatic events in recent Jewish history is almost to step back and say that our history as a People ended after Biblical times. But when we participate in the Modern-Day holidays, it is a testament to our belief that not only does God care about our individual lives, but as a People as well. And not only is He involved in our physical well-being as a People, He is very much involved in our spiritual well-being as well. He is very much involved in our history as He was thousands of years ago, when the Temple once stood and when prophets still walked the streets of Jerusalem.

Yom Hashoah: Holocaust Memorial Day

"Creator of all, Source and shelter, Grant a perfect rest under your tabernacle of peace
To those who perished in the Holocaust, Our fathers and mothers, Our sisters and brothers,
Our rabbis and teachers, Our neighbors and children, the named and the unnamed,
Whose lives were cut off by brutal, vicious, cunning and calculated violence.
May they find peace in the world to come…

Put an end to anger, hatred and fear and lead us to a time when no one will suffer at the hand of another, Speedily, in our days. May the memories of all who faced these horrors

*Be sanctified with joy and love. May their souls be bound up
in the bond of life,
A living blessing in our midst."*

-A Holocaust Prayer for Yom Hashoah

No question has been more perplexing and disturbing to the Modern Jew than the burning question of the Nazi Holocaust of Europe. Six million of our brothers and sisters, including one and a half million children, one third of our People, and two thirds of European Jewry, died at the hands of perhaps the greatest manifestation of evil in world history. The question burns in every thinking Jewish mind at some point in his or her life, and has led countless numbers of Jews to abandon their Jewish heritage, if not abandon God altogether.

The question, has always, and always will be, at least in our lifetime here on this earth, an unanswerable question. Anyone who claims to know the answers is either arrogant, a charlatan, or both. In the words of the *Lubavitcher Rebbe*, "The only answer we can give is: only God knows. However, the very fact that there is no answer to this question is proof that one is not required to know the answer, or understand it, in order to fulfill one's purpose in life. Despite the lack of satisfactory answer to the awesome and tremendous "Why?"- one can, and must, carry on a meaningful and productive life, promote justice and kindness in one's surroundings, and indeed help create a world where there should be no room for any Holocaust, or any kind of man's inhumanity to other man.

As a matter of fact, in the above there is an answer to an unspoken question "What should my reaction be?" The answer to this question must be seen as a challenge to every Jew because Jews were the principal victims of the Holocaust. This challenge should be met head on with all resolve and determination, namely, that regardless how long it will take the world to repent for the Holocaust and make the world a fitting place to live in for all human beings, I, for one, will not slacken in my determination to carry out my purpose in life, which is to serve God wholeheartedly, and with joy, and make this world a fitting abode not only for humans but also for the *Shechina*, the Divine Presence itself."

However, as Jews, we have a commandment to remember. The

Book of Deuteronomy writes "Only guard yourself, and guard your soul carefully, lest you forget the things your eyes saw, and lest these things depart your heart all the days of your life; and you shall make them known to your children and to your children's children." Indeed, a great part of Jewish prayer and ritual is devoted to remembrance. In addition, we are commanded to "Remember that which Amalek did to us." The Nazis, according to many modern-day commentators, are quite possibly descendants, either literally or spiritually of the ancient Amalek tribe, the Biblical archenemies of the Jewish People. Indeed, the Nazi atheistic philosophy of an amoral society was very much in line with the ancient Amalekites. It is often quoted that Hitler said in his book *Mein Kampf* "Conscience is a Jewish invention like circumcision. My task is to free men from the dirty and degrading ideas of conscience and morality." Similarly, elsewhere he said "The struggle for world domination is between me and the Jews. All else is meaningless. The Jews have inflicted two wounds on the world: Circumcision for the body and conscience for the soul. I come to free Mankind from their shackles." This is perhaps the most important reason to remember the Holocaust. It was more than just the death of the Six Million; it was the very real struggle of Good versus Evil, of morality versus amorality.

The Book of Deuteronomy writes "I will surely hide My Face from before you." The Holocaust was the saddest expression of what can occur when God Hides so to speak from using His Providence and Guidance, leaving Man to his own devices. When this occurs, a small segment of humanity strips themselves of that very essence that makes them human.

Are there any positives to learn from the Holocaust? Absolutely. In the same token that the Holocaust showed the depravity that man can sink to, it also showed, perhaps even more so, the extraordinary heights that man can soar to. For every act of evil committed by the Nazis, there were countless numbers of selfless acts done in the camps and ghettos. Jews risked their lives or risked beatings to perform Mitzvot such as donning *Tefillin* (Phylacteries), studying Torah, praying, lighting Chanukah candles, and even fasting on Yom Kippur. There were also incidences of Jews sacrificing their small morsels of food to give to people who were in even worse situations than they themselves were in. In the non-Jewish world, countless numbers of non-Jews risked their lives to save Jews from certain death.

Yes, there existed an Eichmann and a Himmler, but there was also a Raoul Wallenberg and Oscar Schindler. And after the war was over, when the full horrors of the Holocaust were revealed for all of the world to see, there came an outpouring of care and humanitarian support from all over the world. Numerous memorials and museums were opened, and survivor's stories were heard and recorded for the first time. The Eichmann trial became one of the most watched events in television history. The release of Evil into the world brought a tenfold release of Good into the world.

And so, it all becomes a matter of perspective. I thought about this a lot after the 9/11 attacks as well. One can focus on the vile acts of the 19 terrorists and their mastermind Bin Laden, or one can focus on the hundreds of policemen, firemen, and paramedics who rushed into harm's way to save as many lives as they could. One can focus on the extraordinary expression of compassion for the victims' families by millions of people all over the world who prayed for them and sent financial and emotional support.

The Hebrew date which was picked for *Yom Hashoah*, was not just an arbitrary day that was picked. It was right near the day when the famous Warsaw Ghetto Uprising began. Thus, *Yom Hashoah* is not just commemorating the Holocaust, it is also remembering the courageous resistance that many Jews had during that time to stand up to our oppressors and fight for their freedom and dignity.

As Jews living today, we are proud to now carry on what many have called the 614th commandment of the Torah. This is to continue to live as Jews with dignity and honor, and not allow what the Nazis had attempted to do us. We "take revenge" by not allowing Hitler to win. The "Thousand Year Reich" as Hitler once declared, ended in flames and ashes after only 12 miserable years. But we? We continue to light Chanukah candles, and observe the Shabbat. We now have even returned to our homeland after 2,000 years. We continue to pray, to study His Torah. We impart to the next generation the beauty and warmth of our tradition. Let us teach our children not only about the horrors of the Holocaust, but also of what we have today, and the proud Jewish world we have built in its aftermath.

The story is told about a father and son sitting Passover night in the Warsaw ghetto. It came time for the *Mah Nishtana,* the famous Four

Questions that are asked by every Jewish child at the Passover Seder. After asking the Four Questions, the son turned to his father and said he had two additional questions. He asked his father with a trembling little voice "*Abba*, will I be alive next year to ask these questions again? And will you be alive to hear me ask you these questions?" The father, shaking with emotion, answered "I am not a prophet and so I don't know the answer to those questions. However, one thing I do know with absolute certainty is that long after Hitler and the Nazis have disappeared, there will still be Jews sitting at the Passover Seder and plenty of children asking their parents the *Mah Nishtanah*."

This is the story of the Jewish people. Where are the Nazis today? They are Six Feet Under, and the few remnants who try to mimic their actions are considered the vilest people on earth. But as for we the Jews? We keep on living, and not just living but thriving. We have outlived them all, and continue to tell the tale.

Yom Hazikaron: Remembrance Day

"God on High and in our Hearts: Grant reassuring peace beneath the cover of Your Presence to all the men and women who gave their lives in defense of our country and the freedom of the world. Shelter them among the righteous souls who are as radiant as the luminous firmament. Source of Compassion, may we continue to feel their touch on our souls. Hasten the day when peace and security shall prevail, when "nation shall not lift up sword against nation, and there shall be no need to prepare for war." May the day come when the world will stand together as one. May the memory of our fallen brothers and sisters serve as an inspiration to us and as a comfort to all their loved ones. Amen."

-Yom Hazikaron Prayer

One of the greatest aspects of Jewish Tradition is that we never forget. We have a Biblical commandment, as mentioned in the previous section, to never forget that which Amalek did to us. Furthermore, as Jews, we say at each of the three major Biblical holidays the *Yizkor* prayer, which has both a communal section for people who have been murdered just because they were Jews, as well as a personal section for memory of loved ones. The *Kaddish* Prayer is recited for an entire year in memory of a family member who recently passed. Plaques adorn our synagogues and schools that memorialize deceased loved ones. In Israel, when a soldier falls, often thousands of people attend the funeral, including government officials, and the casket is draped in an Israeli flag.

The Talmud teaches us that 3 things are acquired in this world with *Yisurim*, that is with great pain. These three are Torah, the World to Come, and the Land of Israel. Torah has been difficult to learn at many times in our history during times of religious persecution. Acquiring the World to Come often comes with great difficulty, including challenges and discipline and often sacrificing things that may be difficult to give up. And certainly, as we have seen in our times, the Land of Israel, with all its beauty and majesty, has come at a great price.

In Biblical times, there was the sacred concept of *Milchemet Mitzvah*, a war for a holy purpose. In Biblical times wars were to help the Jewish People either conquer or defend the Land of Israel. Many in the contemporary rabbinate feel that the modern-day wars in Israel are again *Milchemet Mitzvah*, a reawakening of a mitzvah that has been dormant for thousands of years. I feel the greatest heroes are those who give up their lives for a noble cause. There is, in my humble opinion, no nobler cause than to die as Jews defending our Holy Land. This is the greatest sanctification of God's Name. Also memorialized on *Yom Hazikaron* are victims of terror attacks, who also died sanctifying God's name, as they were killed just simply because they were Jews living in Israel. To date, over 24,000 Jews have been killed from 1948 till the present day, either in the many wars, or through acts of terror. Much like *Yom Hashoah*, on *Yom Hazikaron* in israel the siren wails for one full minute and the entire country stops. Even cars driving on the highway come to a halt. People step out of their cars and bow their heads in memory of the fallen.

Yom Hazikaron was picked to be the day before *Yom Haatzmaut*, Israel's Independence Day, because to fully appreciate the victory we must first remember the price that needed to be paid. When we appreciate those who have sacrificed their lives for the gift that is the Land of Israel, we come to appreciate the gift even more.

There may be another reason why we commemorate *Yom Hazikaron* before we celebrate *Yom Haatzmaut*. This is because the story of the Jewish People has always been going from tragedy to triumph. It is interesting that in the Torah right after the verse "I will surely hide My Face from you" comes the verse "And now write down this song." What is the connection? Right after one of the saddest verses in the Torah, which according to many commentators, is a reference to the Holocaust, comes an uplifting verse about singing? Who is ready to sing after tragedy? But much like the seasonal cycle of the calendar where spring is preceded by winter, so is the story of the Jewish People. Right after the Holocaust, came the birth of the State of Israel. In biblical times, right after *Tisha B'av*, the saddest day of the Jewish year, the Prophet Isaiah proclaimed the words "*Nachamu Nachamu Ami* (Comfort, comfort My People)" the words of consolation which are read in celebration of *Shabbat Nachamu*. And so, with this spirit in mind, let us turn our attention to the great celebration of *Yom Haatzmaut*.

Yom Haatzmaut: Israel Independence Day

"Open the gates of victory for me that I may
enter then and praise the Lord,
This is the gateway to the Lord, the righteous shall enter through it,
I praise You, for You have answered me, and
have become my deliverance,
The stone that the builders rejected has become the chief cornerstone,
This is the Lord's doing; it is marvelous in our sight,
This is the day that the Lord has made – let us exult and rejoice in it."

-Hallel Prayer recited on Yom Haatzmaut

In World History, there have generally been no comebacks. The Roman Empire, with all its glory and power, fell to the dust, never to return. The Babylonian Empire with all its conquest and grandeur, is now just part of the annals of history, briefly studied in the classroom history books. The mighty Greek Empire,and all its beauty, art, and luster, are now just remnants of an ancient past with relics nothing more than tourist attractions. And so it has been with every other major empire. The Persian Empire, the Turkish Empire, the Byzantine Empire, the Ottoman Empire, etc.

That is, all except one. The Jewish People, once the most treasured and revered people on Earth with their own beautiful Holy Temple, were thrown into exile for nearly 2,000 years from their ancient Biblical Homeland, dispersed throughout the world, and had recently suffered the greatest genocide in human history. And suddenly, miraculously, they returned home.

How could this possibly occur? The Jewish People were given a promise. In the book of Deuteronomy, it is written "The Lord your God will return you to the land that belonged to your ancestors, and you will possess that land again. Then he will make you even more prosperous and numerous than your ancestors." And so, in 1948, it was fulfilled.

To fully appreciate the miracle of the State of Israel, it is important to look at the wondrous events that led to its creation. Let's begin at the post-Holocaust Jewish world. The Jewish People were battered and bruised in ways that they have never been before. Two thirds of European Jewry, one third of the Jewish People had been murdered. The survivors were badly malnourished, beaten, and melancholy. Many had been moved to Displaced Persons camps, such as the ones on the island of Cyprus. Some attempted to return to their homes in Europe, only to find their homes either destroyed or taken over by strangers. Many even faced the same anti-Semitism they had experienced from the Nazis. Only two safe havens remained: The United States and Palestine. While many survivors did in fact go the America, an even greater number found comfort on the shores of their ancient homeland. However, hostilities continued to grow with the local Palestinians as attacks on the small Israeli settlements began to occur with greater frequency and intensity. And so, the desire to create a nation in the ancient Jewish Homeland where they could have autonomy and security from their enemies began to build.

The idea of having a partition, that is, to have two countries, one called Palestine and one called Israel to accommodate both the Arabs and Jews living there, began to grow in popularity amongst the Jews living there. Eventually the matter was brought to the United Nations and voted on there. As hopeful as the Jews were, the chances of getting the resolution for a partition passed was very small. However, many more countries than expected voted in favor of the partition plan. This included, incredibly enough, the Soviet Union, despite the cruel and blatant antisemitism of its brutal dictator Joseph Stalin. The Hidden Divine Hand was turning the pendulum of history toward His Chosen People at last.

And so, on May 14th 1948, the same day the British officially left Palestine, the State of Israel was declared by David Ben Gurion, acting as its provisional Prime Minister. Ben Gurion, who was certainly not a believing Jew by any stretch of the imagination, wrote about the mood right outside of his home just before the Declaration was made: "The Jews of Palestine were dancing because they were about to realize what was one of the most remarkable and inspiring achievements in human history: A people which had been exiled from its homeland two thousand years before, which had endured countless pogroms, expulsions, and persecutions, but which had refused to relinquish its identity—which had, on the contrary, substantially strengthened that identity; a people which only a few years before had been the victim of mankind's largest single act of mass murder, killing a third of the world's Jews, that people was returning home as sovereign citizens in their own independent state." Eleven minutes after the Declaration was made, the United States, one of the world's great superpowers, was the first to recognize the sovereignty of the Jewish State. Indeed, it was arguably the greatest comeback in history.

However, the Arab world was livid at the prospect of Jews having their own homeland within their midst. The day right after the Declaration was made, seven surrounding Arab countries declared war on the new fragile State. And so, the new state, which did not own a single plane, and had a meager "army" which was comprised of mostly Holocaust survivors and farmers was invaded by five well-trained Arab armies. Outnumbered and outgunned, the small Jewish State miraculously not only declared victory, but gained 50% of the land that had been allotted to the Palestinians. However, the war had come at a painful cost. Although the number of Arab casualties was far greater, the new Jewish State had suffered a considerable blow as well. Over 6,000 Jews died during the war, some 2,000 of which were civilians.

But despite the high casualties, the consensus was that the Jewish victory was nothing short of a miracle. One of my favorite stories was that of the Davidka artillery piece, named to remind people of the young fragile King David fighting the mighty giant Goliath. Although the crude weapon had very little accuracy and power, it made a terribly frightening loud noise upon impact, and had enormous psychological effects. During the war over the holy city of Safed, immediately after the Davidka was used, it started to rain. This was especially miraculous since it occurred at a time when it very rarely rains in Israel. The Arab armies, believing the rumor that an Atomic weapon causes it to rain due to changes in atmospheric pressure, believed the Davidka explosion was nothing but the atomic bomb itself. And so, the better trained and better equipped Arab armies, fled, leaving the city in Jewish hands once again.

Understanding and appreciating *Yom Haatzmaut* means not only studying the Torah sources for the importance and religious significance of the Land of Israel, but also appreciating the rich and wondrous history surrounding the creation of our tiny State, and the continuous Divine Spirit which helps to sustain it to this very day. *Rabbi Abraham Isaac Kook,* who did not live through the Independence of Israel, but did live through the Balfour Declaration, was able to see the Divine Providence of the great Jewish return to Israel. He coined the term "Reishit Smichat Geulatenu," that is "the beginning of the flowering of our redemption." Indeed, for we have witnessed not only an extraordinary number of Jews returning, but also Jews returning from all walks of life and places. The Yemenite and Ethiopian Jews, Jews who had been maintaining their ancient Jewish practices for centuries, although seemingly abandoned, came back to Israel. They came to fulfill the ancient Jewish prophecy that the Jewish People will one day return on the "Wings of Eagles." Indeed, not only have we witnessed a great return, but a tiny Jewish State which has isen to the top of the world in technology, innovation, altruism, and democratic values. We have much to be proud of regarding our tiny State, and we have witnessed perhaps the greatest resurgence of Jewish tradition and Torah learning in the new State as well.

Yom Yerushalayim (Jerusalem Day)

"The wells are filled again with water, The square with joyous crowd,
On the Temple Mount within the City, the shofar rings out loud.
Within the caverns in the mountains, A thousand suns will glow,
We'll take the Dead Sea road together, that runs through Jericho.

Oh, Jerusalem of gold, and of light and of bronze,
I am the lute for all your song."

-Jerusalem of Gold Song

No other city has captured the imagination so poignantly of both scholars and poets alike quite like King David's city, the holy City of Jerusalem. It is written in the Talmud that "Ten measures of beauty descended to the world. Of those, Jerusalem took nine." Certainly, in Jewish tradition, no place on earth can compare to the great and mystical city. In the Jewish Bible alone, not counting the Talmud, it is mentioned 669 times. We pray for its complete return three times every day in the Silent Prayer. At the most joyous moment of our lives, standing under the *Chuppah* (marriage canopy) we remember that our joy is still tempered by the knowledge that Jerusalem is still not in its complete state. When we bake *Challah*, we leave one small piece to be burnt in memory of the destruction of Jerusalem. And at the two most climactic moments of the Jewish year; namely at the conclusions of Yom Kippur and the Passover Seder, we sing "Next Year in Jerusalem." Jerusalem is consistently in our thoughts and prayers and captures the yearning of every Jewish soul.

Once again, just like *Yom Haatzmaut*, understanding the history of what occurred on *Yom Yerushalayim* helps us to appreciate its theological significance.

For a moment, let's travel back to June of 1967. The small and fragile Jewish State was once again threatened with annihilation from its surrounding Arab enemies. Abdul Nasser, the leader of Egypt had amassed much of his army at the Sinai border, and closed the Straits of Tiran to Israeli ships, considered by Israel to be an act of war. Nasser also signed an alliance with Syria and Jordan to once and for all, as he put it, "drive the Zionist enemy into the Mediterranean Sea." The State of Israel was to be a 19-year dream, and would soon become a faded memory. To say the Arab legions had the upper hand would be a cruel understatement, not only was Israel outnumbered and severely outgunned, but Israel's relatively small air force was no match for Egypt's vast and sophisticated, Russian-supplied, air power. In Israel, the threat was considered so severe, that space in national and local parks were set aside for the mass graves expected from the oncoming onslaught.

But alas, once again, as in the War for Independence of 1948, God had very different plans for the Jewish State. Israeli Intelligence learned of a small window of time when the Egyptian Air Force pilots ate breakfast and all their planes were on the ground. On early morning June 5th, flying at an extremely low altitude to avoid radar detection, nearly all of the Israeli Air Force set out on a daring mission; to launch a preemptive strike and destroy as much of the Egyptian air force as they could on the ground. Incredibly, not only were weather conditions for such a mission just perfect, but astoundingly, nearly every missile fired by Israel hit with a precision never seen before in the practice raids. In only four hours, almost the entire Egyptian Air Force was destroyed on the ground with no Israeli casualties. In a matter of hours, the tables had turned.

But Israel wasn't finished. Now with the air superiority, Israel began to drive the Egyptian army out of their offense position along the Sinai border. Incredibly, in a very short time, Israel managed to drive the Syrian army out of Sinai and capture the entire Sinai Peninsula. And the miracles were far from over. Jordan and Syria, having listened to false propaganda from Nasser that Egypt was winning the war, began launching attacks on Israel, leading Israel to counter-attack and drive them out from the West Bank and Gaza, which included the conquer of the holy City of Hebron with the Tomb of the Patriarchs. Once thought to be well-trained and organized armies, they showed complete chaos and dysfunction and Israel easily defeated them. But the final and perhaps greatest miracle of all, came on the final day of the war, with the fight for

East Jerusalem, with the Old City and the most prized possession of all, the Western Wall. *General Moshe Dayan* ordered no live ammunition be used by Israel, only rubber bullets, in deference to the Old City's holy sites, which automatically put the Israeli army at a disadvantage militarily. But miraculously the Jordanian army fled, offering very little resistance. And once again, the entire Jerusalem, complete with the revered *Kotel Maravi*, the Western Wall, was in Jewish hands. *"Har Habayit beyadenu:* The Temple Mount is in our hands!" became the rallying cry of the time. One of the most powerful recordings, in my opinion is the live news report of the capturing of the Western Wall, where one can hear gunshots in the background, but more importantly, the sounds of the soldiers singing and weeping as they approached the Western Wall. Everyone reported something electric was in the air. Something magical and most certainly miraculous had just taken place. Something our ancestors had only dreamed of had just become a reality.

Although the Jewish People paid a price during the war, it was nowhere near the extremely heavy toll that took place to the Arab legions. Less than 1,000 Israelis were killed compared to over 20,000 Arabs, with much of their artillery and morale completely crushed. To this day, the Israeli wars are not studied in many military schools, including West Point, due to the wars completely defying logic from the normal course of how wars are fought and won. Yet, still, sadly enough, the Arab world remained defiant. Although the Israeli government offered an olive branch of peace, the Arab world refused. In September of 1967, the Arab League Summit declared its infamous "Three No's," that is No to recognition, No to Peace, and No to negotiations with Israel. And so the conflict remains to this day.

One last point to be made about Yom Yerushalayim, and the Six Day War in general. I wrote this book specifically to be inspirational without any political views discussed, but here and only here, I feel compelled to make one very important point. Sadly enough, many people today, and some even of our own brothers and sisters, try to paint Israel as the aggressors who have been conducting an unlawful "occupation" of the conquered territories ever since the Six Day War. While I strongly believe Israel should always try to give as much freedom as possible to the Palestinian people, it must always be remembered that The Six

Day War, *was a war of self-defense*, and nothing else. The choice was either launch preemptive strikes or face complete annihilation. And the continued military presence and security wall has helped to thwart literally thousands of potential terrorist attacks over the years and has led to the arrest of thousands of terrorists who either harmed or meant to harm innocent Israelis. It must also be remembered that on at least two occasions Israel has offered to give back nearly all of the land it had won in exchange for peace, and both times the offers were refused. In addition, the Palestinian people had, in recent years, voted Hamas into power, and the Palestinian Authority still gives large stipends to the families of terrorists. Terrorists who murdered innocent people are still lauded as heroes in these areas by most Palestinians as streets are named after them and billboards are hung up, celebrating their "achievements." With this mindset, unfortunately, it has been very difficult to achieve a lasting peace with them.

There. I have said my piece. Time to step away from politics for now and continue with the inspirational message of this book. May we all continue to appreciate the great gift that is Jerusalem, and may we continue to bask in its eternal beauty. And may we live to see it fully rebuilt speedily in our times.

Spiritual Exercises

1. For *Yom Hashoah*:
   A. Take some time on this day to learn a little more about the Holocaust. Also take a few minutes to study the life of one person who perished in the Holocaust. There are plenty of available resources online for this. Try to pick someone who was about your age so you can relate more to that person.
   B. Try to take a few minutes to watch online the story of one survivor. Seeing and hearing from someone who experienced the horror helps to make the Holocaust feel more real.
   C. Take a minute for a moment of silence for the victims of the Holocaust. Also take a moment to reflect on the pitfalls on intolerance and where hatred can lead. Think of how you can be more inclusive and loving toward other minority groups.

2. For *Yom Hazikaron*:
   A. Take a few minutes to learn about any of the wars that Israel has fought for its security. Take a minute to learn about one person who has died for Israel, either a soldier or a victim of a terror attack. Try to find someone close to your age so you can relate to that person better.
   B. Take a minute for a moment of silence on this day to remember the fallen soldiers and victims of terror. Try to think about the sacrifice they have made for our Holy Land and our People. And say a prayer for peace one day in the Holy Land.

3. For *Yom Haatzmaut*:
   A. Take some time to learn the history of the early State of Israel, and the pioneers who helped to make it happen. Learn the religious significance of the modern-day State, and study some words of Torah about the special uniqueness of the Land of Israel.

B. Go to a celebration on Yom Haatzmaut in honor of this day. Whether a musical performance, or Israel-themed movie or speech, or even eating Israeli food are great ways to honor the special nature of the day. Listen to some of the many beautiful songs online about Israel. Dressing in blue and white, the colors of the Israeli flag, is a great way to show Israeli pride.

4. For *Yom Yerushalayim:*
   A. Take some time to learn the rich history of Jerusalem, from Biblical times till the present day. Learn a little more about the enormous religious and spiritual significance of Jerusalem.
   B. Go to a celebration on *Yom Yerushalayim.* Try to go to one that is especially joyous, maybe one with live music. Pick one that commemorates both the historical and spiritual significance of that day.
   C. Try to think of ways to connect to Jerusalem in a more meaningful way on a regular basis. Maybe listen to songs or buy a book about the spiritual and physical beauty of Jerusalem. Or hang up paintings or photos of Jerusalem in your home.

The Fiery Embers of Lag Baomer

"Bar Yochai - fortunate are you, anointed with joyous oil [i.e. wisdom], over and above your companions.

Bar Yochai...You were anointed with the holy oil that flows down from the transcendent source of mercy. Like the High Priest, you wore a holy crown that set you aside from other men, an aura of splendor bound eternally upon your head.

Bar Yochai...It was a comely dwelling that you found, on the day you ran away and escaped from the Romans. For thirteen years you stood in the sand of the rocky cave - there you merited to your crown of splendor and radiance.

Bar Yochai...Your students are like the strong and beautiful beams of acacia wood used to hold up the Tabernacle. When they learn G-d's Torah, they become ignited with the wondrous burning light of its secrets. Behold, these secrets were revealed to you by your teachers Moses and Elijah."

-Lag Baomer Song

PERHAPS THE MOST MYSTICAL DAY of the Jewish calendar is known as *Lag Baomer*; which is simply translated as the 33rd day of the Omer, in the count leading up to *Shavuot*. This is a day celebrated with great festivity by Jews throughout the world, but especially in the Land of Israel. Two events are celebrated on Lag Baomer. These two events are 1) the ending of a plague which killed 24,000 students of the great Talmudic Sage Rabbi Akiva and 2) the death of a great Talmudic sage and founder of Kabbalah, Rabbi Shimon Bar Yochai. It was on the final day of his life when he was said to get his greatest mystical secrets. On the day of his death, bar Yochai said, "Now it is my desire to reveal secrets... The day will not go to its place like any other, for this entire day stands within my domain..." Daylight was miraculously extended until he had completed his final teaching and died. As such, the custom of lighting fires on his *Yahrzeit* (anniversary of death) symbolizes this revelation of powerful light.

The two great Talmudic personalities associated with Lag Baomer will be the focus of this chapter, as well as the correlations between them and the events we commemorate on this great day. Let us take a moment to examine these two great people and their own very unique life stories.

Let us examine Rabbi Shimon Bar Yochai first. He was born, according to the Talmud, into very miraculous circumstances. His parents were Sarah and Yochai and were barren for nearly ten years. According to Jewish Tradition, a husband and wife are to get divorced if they remain childless for ten years. Sarah overheard her husband speaking with great sadness to his colleagues about his plans to divorce her. That night she cried bitter tears from a very broken heart. That night, her husband Yochai had a dream. In it, there was a forest filled with many beautiful trees. However, he was standing in front of a very withered, dead tree. A gardener was going around with a giant bucket and was watering all of the trees. When he reached the tree that Yochai was standing in front of, he reached into his pocket and pulled out a little flask. When he poured out the liquid from this flask onto this tree, the tree suddenly grew and blossomed into a tree far more beautiful than any other tree in the garden. When Yochai awoke, he went to the great sage Rabbi Akiva and asked him the meaning of the dream. He explained that the withered tree was their own barren state they were in, but they will soon have a son who will grow up to be one of the greatest and most righteous Torah scholar that the world will ever see. When he asked Rabbi Akiva what was in the flask that the gardener pulled out to water the withered tree, Rabbi Akiva responded it was his wife's tears that she shed last night. And so it was, the great Rabbi

Shimon Bar Yochai was soon born. Rabbi Shimon was soon to study under Rabbi Akiva and become his greatest disciple. In fact, when the 24,000 students of Rabbi Akiva perished, only five students remained, who would be tasked with spreading Torah to the rest of the world. One of these five students was none other than Rabbi Shimon Bar Yochai.

Rabbi Akiva's name is perhaps more familiar to everyone since we have a rendezvous each year with him at the Passover Seder in the Haggadah. He is one of the five sages mentioned in the Haggadah who spend the entire Passover night discussing the story of the Exodus, until one of their students came and informed them it is time for the morning prayers.

Rabbi Akiva's birth was extraordinary as well, but it is a different type of birth we are discussing here, namely the birth of his Jewish faith. Rabbi Akiva, according to the Talmud, came from humble beginnings. He was born completely irreligious, and according to the Talmud, even anti-religious, stating a complete disdain, perhaps even hatred for Torah scholars. He was a shepherd by trade; a profession known at the time to be one which was involved in uncouth behavior. However, he found a good woman who went against her father's wishes and married him, for she saw a positive spark in him that no one else did. However, according to the Talmud, Rabbi Akiva's life dramatically changed when he one day saw water dripping onto a rock. The water, which may have been dripping for hundreds, perhaps thousands of years, bore a hole into the rock. He had an epiphany, and said to himself, "if drops of water can pierce through a rock, maybe the words of Torah, which is compared to water, can pierce through the rock which is my heart?" And so it was, with the encouragement and self-sacrifice of his loving wife, he set off to study Torah. Many years later, he emerged as one of the greatest sages of the Talmud and had amassed over 24,000 students.

Rabbi Shimon Bar Yochai spent many years hiding from the Romans, and studying Torah, a practice which would have cost him his life. Legend has it, according to the Talmud, Rabbi Shimon Bar Yochai hid for 12 years in a cave from the Romans, miraculously living off a carob tree planted just outside the cave. And Rabbi Akiva also spent many years hiding from the Romans so he could study Torah. When asked why he risked his life in such a way, answered with a parable:

"Imagine a school of fish swimming away from a fisherman's net. A fox watches this, and slyly says to the fish, why don't you come onto the dry land here with me where you will be safe from the fisherman's nets? The fish replied "you are foolish, and we could see your slyness. If here in the water, which is the only place we can live, our lives are in danger, how much more so on dry land, where we cannot survive, our lives will be in danger!" Rabbi Akiva explains that Torah is the force that gives our souls life, as it is written in the verse "With it you will live, and your days will be lengthened." How much more so would our souls, which help to give our lives meaning, be in danger, if we were not to study Torah! To me, this parable is even more poignant, in that once again he used the analogy of water, as the Torah is compared to water many times. Water is what drew him into Judaism (when he saw water dripping on the rock) and water is what kept him into Judaism, despite the dangers at the time.

Rabbi Akiva's end is perhaps the most tragic but also inspiring story in all of Talmud. The punishment for Torah study under Roman rule was certain death. The Roman Emperor Tineius Rufus ordered his execution in the Hippodrome in Caesarea. According to Jewish tradition, he was tortured to death, skinned alive, and nevertheless recited the Shema, as the time to recite the Shema had arrived. When his students asked him how he was able to recite the Shema at such a time. He answered them, "All my life I was worried about the verse, 'with all your soul' (and the sages expounded this to signify), even if He takes away your soul. And I said to myself, when will I ever be able to fulfill this command? And now that I am finally able to fulfill it, I should not?" Then he extended the final word *Echad* ("One") until his life expired with that word. A heavenly voice went out and announced: "Blessed are you, *Rabbi* Akiva, that your life expired with "*Echad*." Having died a true martyr's death, according to the Talmud a Heavenly Voice continued "You will sit next to the Throne of Glory for all eternity." Rabbi Akiva is buried in the holy city of Tiberias in Israel alongside many other great sages.

Both Rabbi Akiva and Rabbi Shimon Bar Yochai seemed to appreciate and understand not only the more revealed aspects of Torah, but the hidden aspects as well. Rabbi Shimon Bar Yochai was a great sage of the Talmud and was often involved in the discussions pertaining to Jewish Law. However, he was of course most well-known for being the spiritual father of Kabbalah, the secrets of Jewish Wisdom contained in the Torah. Indeed, he was believed by many in the Jewish tradition to have authored the *Zohar* (Book of Splendor), which is considered to be the preeminent book of Kabbalah. And Rabbi Akiva was known according to one Midrash to be able to understand even the *crowns* which sit on top of the Hebrew letters in the Torah, and what their deeper meaning was, a feat which even *Moshe* (Moses) was unable to do. Perhaps even more telling of Rabbi Akiva's tremendous prowess in the secrets of Torah is the legendary story of the *Pardes*, recorded in the Talmud. The story of the *Pardes* is a very cryptic one, which has been the subject of many interpretations throughout the ages. According to the story, four great Talmudic Sages were transported to *Pardes*, which literally means an orchard. According to some interpretations, this was a spiritual Paradise, perhaps Heaven. Others interpret it to mean that the Hebrew word "Pardes" stands for the acronym *Pshat, Remez, Drash,* and *Sod*. These are the four levels of understanding the Torah, *Sod* being the deepest most mystical of the four ways to understand Torah. This is the Kabbalah. These four Talmudic Sages were Rabbi Akiva, Ben Zoma, Ben Azzai, and Acher. Three of these four sages could not handle the full and deepest understanding of the Torah. One died, another went insane, the third became a heretic. Only Rabbi Akiva, the Talmud says "Entered in peace, and left in peace." Only he was able to grasp the fullest and deepest meanings of the Torah and remain completely intact; physically, mentally, and spiritually.

Rabbi Akiva had a deep love for the Jewish People and saw their unique bond with their Creator. He once famously declared "Praiseworthy is the Jewish People! Just as the *Mikvah* (ritual bath) purifies those who are impure, so too The Holy One Blessed Be He purifies the Jewish People." He had an infinite hope in his People and he never lost site of the fact that treating one's fellow man with honor and respect was of complete paramount, even more than the other precepts in the Torah. "Loving one's fellow Man as one loves Oneself-This is the greatest precept in the entire Torah." Sadly, enough, this concept did not penetrate to his students, many of whom died from a plague because, as the Talmud teaches, they could not treat each other with proper respect.

Rabbi Shimon Bar Yochai at first seemed to hold a very different outlook. He was the one who famously argued with another Talmudic Sage regarding the importance of Torah study and worldly occupation. While Rabbi Yishmael saw the importance of working in the fields as part of living a complete life when it is in conjunction with Torah study, Rabbi Shimon Bar Yochai had a different view entirely. He declared "Is working really possible? If a man plows in the plowing season, and sows in the sowing season, and reaps in the reaping season, and threshes in the threshing season, and winnows in the season of wind, what is to become of the Torah? No, but when Israel perform the will of the Omnipresent their work is performed by others, as it is stated: "And strangers shall stand and feed your flocks." He believed it is better for others to take care of a Jew's needs so that he may immerse himself completely in Torah study. He was wont to quote the well-known verse "The words of Torah shall not leave your lips," that is that Torah study took precedence over all else.

When Rabbi Shimon emerged from the cave, he seemed to have become even more extreme. When he saw people involved in the mundane activities of the world, such as farming, or tilling the land for livelihood, he could not tolerate the seeming pettiness of their lives. According to Talmudic legend, he would gaze upon their land that they were toiling, and it would burn up before his very eyes. Finally, a Heavenly Voice came out and said "Rabbi Shimon, is this why you have come out of my cave? To destroy my creations?" Legend has it, he went back into the cave for twelve months, and when he emerged the next time, he was able to tolerate people and accept them and respect them, even if they were not on his lofty spiritual level. In the end, he was able to glean much of his *Rebbi's* (teacher's) openness, and respectfulness toward others. He famously stated in the Talmud that "It is better to jump into a fiery furnace than to embarrass another in public." And he even started looking at one who finds grace in the eyes of others through good character as the greatest trait of all, even greater than Torah study. In *Pirkei Avot* (Ethics of our Fathers) he declared "There are three crowns: the crown of the Torah, and crown of priesthood, and the crown of royalty; but the crown of a good name excels above them all."

And so, it was that Rabbi Akiva and Rabbi Shimon Bar Yochai emerged from their cocoon of intense Torah study at first with very different perspectives on life, but in the end, both were very much the same. And so, it was that both Rabbi Akiva and Rabbi Shimon Bar Yochai both underwent life changing transformations. Both understood and appreciated the very deep, mystical aspects of the Torah and understood spiritual purity. However, both were also able to understand and see the beauty of their fellow man, even if they were not on a lofty spiritual level. Both contained a boundless optimism in life and humanity. On Lag Baomer, let us take some time to appreciate these two giant luminaries and their incredible legacies they have left behind, legacies that are still felt to this day.

A Lag Baomer Story

The year was 1923. An enormous crowd had gathered in Meron, on the outskirts of Safed to pay tribute to the great *Tzaddik* (righteous one) Rabbi Shimon Bar Yochai, whom many revere as the founder of Kabbalah. All through the night, Chassidim danced to the sway of lively Jewish music, in front of the twirling flames of the large bonfires. The men danced on the roof of the tomb of Rabbi Shimon and his son, while the women and children danced with great energy below in the courtyard. Jews of all walks of life and ages participated in the annual festivities.

One of the highlights of Lag Ba'Omer in Meron was always the *Upsherring* of three year old boys. *Upsherring* was a haircut given to boys at 3 years old and was a custom that had deep Chassidic and Kabbalistic meaning and symbolism. At the ceremony, friends and relatives would pass along the scissors, each taking part in cutting one lock of the young boy's hair.

This particular year Lag Baomer fell on a Thursday night. Jews who had come from afar stayed throughout Shabbat, and special provisions were made. The wonderful festive atmosphere continued throughout Shabbat, with dancing and prayers continuing throughout the day.

But suddenly, a loud wail shattered the glowing atmosphere of Shabbat joy. A little boy, who had come with his mother for his *Upsherring*, had suddenly stopped breathing. Despite attempts to revive the boy, he was soon pronounced dead. In a moment, all the joy that was felt suddenly evaporated, and was replaced with sobbing and melancholy. As word, spread, the mother's pain was palpable to all of those present. In addition, the British soldiers who were guarding the tomb suddenly locked the gates to the tomb. They became paranoid that the boy had died from a contagious disease and could be infecting others as well.

The mob surrounding the tomb suddenly split like the parting of the Red Sea, as the mother of this little boy stormed to the gates of the tomb. Incredibly, the soldiers, perhaps moved by her tears, let her inside. From inside, all of those near the tomb were able to hear her desperate plea.

"Rabbi Shimon! I know of your holiness and compassion, and I beg of you, I beseech you, please pray to the Almighty on my behalf! I love my son dearly! We have come here to honor you. He is my only child. The last three years, I have looked forward to bringing him here. I cannot leave here without my son. Please help to bring back my beloved son!"

She left her child in the tomb and walked out. In a few minutes, all who were nearby suddenly heard a weak timid child's voice from inside of the tomb. "Mommy, mommy, where are you? I am so thirsty. Do you have some water please?"

Everyone present was shaken to the core. They had just witnessed nothing short of a miracle. The great *Tzaddik* Rabbi Shimon Bar Yochai had prayed on this mother's behalf, and indeed, the child had returned to life. The mother burst back into the tomb, and the two of them hugged and sobbed for a long time. The bewildered British soldiers once again opened the gates for all to enter. Soon the singing and dancing began, but this time even more jubilantly than ever before. For they had just witnessed firsthand the greatness of Rabbi Shimon Bar Yochai.

Spiritual Exercises

1. Try to remember a time when you felt really inspired by a song. Which song was it? What inspired you about it? Perhaps start doing searches online for Jewish music that inspires you and connects you to God. Make this music a part of your daily life in addition to the other music you like.

2. Try to take some time each day to study some of the more mystical aspects of Judaism. There are plenty of resources online. Understanding some of the deeper more Kabbalistic understandings of Judaism can certainly enhance your own Jewish experiences.

3. Remember the reason for the plague which affected Rabbi Akiva's students; that they did not treat each other with proper respect. Many times, we are guilty of doing this as well. Think of people in our lives that we may not have treated properly and think of how we can change our attitudes and actions toward those people.

4. Take some time on Lag Baomer to attend a Lag Baomer event. Just about every Jewish community will have an event. Preferably one with live Jewish music and with a bonfire. Look at the fire and see not only its physical light, but its spiritual light as well. It is a wonderful way to connect to the Holiday itself and make it more meaningful.

Shavuot: Receiving the Book of Love

"Were the sky a parchment made
A quill each reed, twig and blade
Could we with ink the oceans fill,
Were every man a scribe of skill,
The marvelous story
Of God's great glory
Would still remain untold;
For he, Most High,
The earth and sky
Created alone of old."
-Shavuot Prayer

OVER 3300 YEARS AGO, THE Jewish people received the greatest Divine Revelation ever recorded in the history of Mankind; the Sinai Revelation. The Bible is very clear about not only the significance of the Revelation, but the unprecedented nature of it. It is written *'You might inquire about times long past, from the day that God created man on earth, and from one end of heaven to the other: Has there ever been anything like this great thing or has anything like it been heard? Has a people ever heard the voice of God speaking from the midst of the fires as you have heard and survived?' (Deut. 4:32-33)* Indeed, never has any other religion made such a claim, and the Sinai Revelation remains the most unique event in human history; and one that is impossible to be fabricated. To this day, the Sinai Revelation is the bedrock of not only the Jewish faith, but of all three monotheistic faiths. Many of the stories, principles, and values of the Jewish Bible have become the cornerstone of most of the civilized world.

Every year, on the holiday of Shavuot, we commemorate this great historic event. However, as we have explained in our travels through Jewish history and time, this holiday, like all the others, does not only commemorate this awesome event, it awakens us to re-experience it. And even more so, particularly for this holiday, it is a moment not only to re-experience, but to reconnect with the deeper messages of the holiday and take those messages with us throughout the year. So, what are these deeper messages? And how is the Torah relevant to us today, in the 21st century?

To have a greater understanding of the significance of this holiday we must analyze the Holiday itself. There are many puzzling aspects to this Holiday. First and foremost is the name of the Holiday, which simply means "Weeks." This is a reference to the seven weeks, known as the Omer, which are counted from the second day of Pesach (Passover) which led up to this holiday. Couldn't there be a more inspiring name for this very important holiday? And furthermore, there seem to be no rituals or commandments associated with the holiday. All other holidays have associated commandments; on Passover we are commanded to eat Matzah, on Sukkot we are commanded to dwell in a Sukkah, etc. And yet this Holiday has no rituals associated with it! Furthermore, the verses in the Torah which discuss the Holiday don't even mention that it is to commemorate the giving of the Torah! The verses only speak about the references to the Harvest season; as a special sacrifice was brought on Shavuot in Temple times that was different than what was brought on Pesach, the holiday which proceeds Shavuot. On Pesach we would bring a sacrifice of barley, while on Shavuot we brought one made of wheat. What is the reason for this distinction? Why is Pesach represented by barley whereas Shavuot is represented by wheat?

To begin to answer these questions we need to start with the days leading up to Shavuot. The period leading up to Shavuot is the well-known period we call *Sefirat Haomer*. What makes this period different from typical counting to an anticipated event is that instead of counting *down* to the event, we count *up*. What is the reason for this? The mystics explain that when it comes to Shavuot, we are not merely *anticipating* an upcoming holiday, rather we are *preparing* for the upcoming holiday. Each day is an opportunity for self-growth, meant to build on the previous day. Therefore, in Kabbalah each of the days of counting is assigned a very specific character trait for on each of these days as we are ideally trying to work to achieve that trait. It is also by no coincidence that *Pirkei Avot* (Ethics of our Fathers) lists 48 ways to acquire wisdom, for it is believed that each of these ways is to be conquered on one of the days leading up to the Holiday of Shavuot when we acquire the Torah, and there are 48 full days between the two holidays.

Let us now return to the question regarding why Passover's sacrifice is with barley and Shavuot's sacrifice is with wheat. Barley is a course type of grain and is one of the most common foods fed to animals. Humans however, are more refined, and largely eat products made from wheat. The Talmud itself says that barley is better fit for animal consumption, while wheat is better fit for human consumption.

So why is Passover represented with a food fit for animals? The Midrash teaches that when the Jewish People left Egypt, they were on the 49th level of impurity. As much as the Talmud tells us they kept such things as their names, language, and clothing separate from the Egyptians, they were still steeped in Egypt's religious practices. The Midrash tells us that if they were to descend one more level, they would have been unredeemable. So the fifty day period leading up to Shavuot was in reality an ascension of spiritual levels, just as it is for Jews today, so they would be worthy of receiving the Divine light contained in the Torah. It was only on Shavuot that they became fully *human,* they receive a spark of the Divine, and are now different from the animal Kingdom. This was symbolized by the special sacrifice on Shavuot of wheat, instead of barley.

Now we can go back and answer our other questions. The Talmud teaches us that the Sinai Revelation when the first Shavuot occurred was on the Sabbath. Even the word "Shavuot" contains the root letters "Shin" Bet" and "Tuf," the same letters of the word "Shabbat." What is the significance of this? The Sabbath as we know is the pinnacle of the week, it is not the state of *becoming* that we experience during the work week, but rather the state of *being.* On the Sabbath, there is no more anticipating or preparing, rather it is the state of having finally *arrived.* So it is with the holiday of Shavuot. The anticipation is over, the great moment in time has finally arrived. The Jewish People have prepared themselves, and the time has come for the great encounter with the Divine. It is for this reason that there are no required rituals associated with the day. It is just a day of being, a day of enjoying a state of Divine Bliss. No rituals are required. On the Sabbath as well, there are no required rituals on the day itself, just sanctification with wine when the Sabbath begins and ending that sanctification when the Sabbath ends. Sabbath too, like Shavuot is a state of being, a rendezvous with the Divine. The three root letters of both Shabbat and Shavuot spell "Tashev" which means "to dwell." For in both we have reached the end of our Journey. In both we are now dwelling in the Presence of the Divine. Both are the culmination of a cycle of seven, seven weeks for Shavuot and seven days for Shabbat. Both Shabbat and Shavuot are compared to a wedding, the wedding between the Jewish people and their Father in Heaven. There are no coincidences in the Hebrew Language or in Judaism, all have a place and a purpose. This is part of the beauty of our Tradition.

Shavuot: The Original State

When the Torah was given, the Jewish People were warned not to ascend the mountain when Moses had ascended Mount Sinai. In fact, the Torah warns this twice, including a warning to not even touch the mountain lest the People would die since their earthly bodies would not be able to handle the Presence of the Divine. The question is, why was there such a powerful urge for the Jewish People to ascend the mountain so that they had to be warned not once, but twice, especially if it meant certain death?

I read a beautiful answer from *Rabbi Ben Tzion Shafier.* He quotes the great commentator *Rashi* who writes "because of their deep desire to receive God, they might attempt to ascend the mountain." He explains that the natural state of a human being is to cling to the Divine. Children are born so simple, pure and innocent, untouched by the bitterness and lusts of the world. The soul has a burning desire to cling to the Divine as a piece of metal would to a magnet. It is our physicality, when it is

133

unfortunately strengthened over the years, that blocks the pull of this Divine Magnet, until some of us don't feel that pull at all. Our purpose in the world is to constantly work to remove those physical barriers that our bodies create and return to the natural state of our souls, that is, to once again cling to the Divine.

The spiritual state of the Jewish People after they had spent the time preparing for Mount Sinai was once again this original state of the soul, completely unblocked by their physical bodies. In fact, the Talmud writes that their spiritual state was just like Adam's state before he ate from the tree, that is, a natural state of closeness to God with no internal desire to sin. The Talmud further writes that the entire Jewish People were on a level of prophecy at that moment. When a person receives prophecy, he or she is engaging in a direct communication with God, with all obstacles removed.

Perhaps the lesson of Shavuot is that by studying Torah we too can experience this at least to a certain degree. By studying His Word, we are little by little removing these obstacles of the physical world and once again receiving communication from the Divine. It is for this reason I believe that Torah has the ability to change someone. No other intellectual subject seems to have this ability. One can study the many great wisdoms in the world, from biology to mathematics to physics, and as fascinating and deep as these subjects may be, the person spiritually and ethically remains the same. Not so with the study of Torah. Countless Jews all over the world throughout the millennia have experienced this firsthand; a moral and spiritual shift due to delving deeply into Torah study. The Talmud writes that the same God who created the Evil Inclination also created the Torah as its *Tavlin*. Many commentators translate the word *Tavlin* to mean "antidote," meaning it is the "cure" so to speak for the evil inclination. However, *Rashi* translates *Tavlin* literally, which means "spices." What does this mean? Often a food that doesn't taste good just needs a little spice to enhance its flavor. So too it is with the Evil Inclination. Although it is a struggle to overcome, and always will be, at least the Torah can make the struggle *easier*, can add just the right spice to make the challenges easier to swallow, to enable our ability to overcome. For through Torah study, we can return to our original state, a state of purity.

As we mentioned before, the Holiday is called *Shavuot,* which contains the root letters *Tuf, Shin, and Bet.* Besides Tashev, which means "to dwell" as we discussed before, it also means "Return." These are the same root letters for the word Teshuvah (Repentance.) For through Torah study we return to the root source of who we are. Similarly, this applies to Shabbat as well. For Shabbat is an oasis in time, it is a moment when we return to the root source of who we are.

It is interesting to note that very little of the Holiday of Shavuot concerns itself with the actual Revelation of Mount Sinai. Rather, it concerns itself with actual Torah study. This is because the Sinai Revelation is only one moment in history; it is the continuous study and practice that makes it relevant and meaningful to our lives. *Rabbi Joseph Ber Soloveitchik* used to say that there are two famous mountains in the Torah, Mount Sinai and the Temple Mount. Mount Sinai, the site of the greatest revelation in human history, is now nowhere to be found, as we do not even know its precise location. However, the site of the Binding of Isaac later became the Temple Mount where both Jewish temples stood, and today is the most revered place on earth. Why is this? Because the Sinai Experience was just one moment of Revelation, of God reaching out to Man. But the Binding of Isaac, was Man's act, Man *choosing* to reach up to God. Man's actions have infinitely more meaning than even actions by the Almighty Himself. The Torah, as Pireki Avot (Ethics of our Fathers) teaches, is to lead, to teaching, which in turn, leads to action. And *action*, it teaches, is the most paramount of all of them.

Often, in Rabbinic exegesis, the Sinai Revelation is compared to a wedding. That is, the great "wedding" so to speak, of the Jewish People to their Father in Heaven. But, of course the wedding is only one day. Anyone who only dreams of the wedding and nothing after that is missing the whole point. The wedding is only one day, in a flash it is over. But the marriage? The marriage lasts a lifetime (hopefully.) So too with Shavuot. The Sinai Revelation was only the initial bonding, it is the daily Torah study that continuously builds our relationship with God.

There is a well-known statement in the Talmud that says God looked into the Torah and then created the world. What does this mean? Some people believe this means that the Torah was the blueprint of creation. I don't believe that this is the case for the Torah was never meant to be a science book and there is very little in it concerning the actual creation of matter, let alone the physics and biology etc. of the complex world we live in. Rather, I believe this statement was meant to teach us that the Torah is a book of theology. While science is concerned with the *how*, the Torah is concerned with the *why*. God first gazed into the Torah, for this would become the wellspring which would give the physical world around us meaning. I believe that God, in His infinite Wisdom, understood that the *purpose* had to be created first, and then the project would follow. And so He designed a world that would give us endless possibilities to find meaning, and through studying the Torah we can find where to look in the world, and what actions will draw us closer to Him and which will pull us away.

The Torah is our moral compass in the world. We live in a world of relative moralism; that is ever changing values and norms. What was once unacceptable behavior now in certain places is not only condoned but sometimes even encouraged. What is acceptable depends on both societal norms and individual feelings or intuitions. This leads to not only moral decay, but also to confusion and chaos. In some societies today even murder, rape, and incest are acceptable in certain situations. The only way to escape the downward spiral that all too often exists in the world today is to submit to a higher Moral Authority. Only the Being with Infinite Wisdom can determine what is right and wrong, and directives for how to live. These directives are contained in the Torah. For without it, we are truly lost.

The Significance of Three

In the Talmud, there is an enigmatic passage: "Blessed be the Merciful One who gave a threefold Torah to a threefold People through a thirdborn son in the third month in the third day." What does this mean, and what is the significance here of the number three?

The Written Torah as we know is divided into three parts: Torah, Prophets, and Writings. It was given to the Jewish People, who consist of three groups, the Priests, the Levites, and the Israelites. The Torah was given through Moses, the thirdborn child of Yocheved. The Torah was given in the Hebrew month of Sivan, the third month of the year. And it was given on the third day of ritual cleanliness from the Jewish People abstaining from marital relations. But again, what is the significance of this number three?

The *Lubavitcher Rebbe* gives a beautiful answer. He explains that the number three signifies a synthesis. The first month of the year was Nissan, redemption from Egypt. This month signifies fleeing from the world as we know it, as the Jewish People escaped from their bondage of slavery. The second month of Iyar represents the Omer, for it is the month entirely of counting, a month of preparation. It is a month of reaching up to God but remaining detached from this world. However, in the month of Sivan, we come to the realization that we can in fact have a dual role; we can cling to God and yet remain attached to this world. The Torah represents this synthesis, it is a path to develop a relationship with God but very much remaining here in this world.

I would like to take this idea one step further. I believe this idea of three can also be seen in the personality of the Patriarchs. As we all know, there are three Patriarchs, Abraham, Isaac, and Jacob. Abraham represented in the Oral Tradition the trait of *Chesed*, that is, of kindness. The month of Nissan best represented this, for it was the month when God did the greatest act of kindness in our history, through open miracles he redeemed us from centuries of bitter slavery. The second Patriarch, Isaac, is represented with the trait of *Din*, that is Judgement. This too is representative of the month of Iyar, for it is an entire month of preparation, of character refinement. And finally, we come to the third Patriarch, that is Jacob. Jacob represented the trait of *Tifferet*, that is the trait of synthesis. It is the trait of harmony between these two very opposing worlds. This is the month of Sivan, the month of synthesis of these two worlds. And this was the month of the giving of the Torah. And incredibly, which Patriarch is the Torah named for? It is named for Jacob! "Torah was commanded to us through Moses, it is an inheritance of *Jacob*" as the Torah writes! Jacob, who dedicated fourteen years of his life to Torah study as the Torah tells us. Jacob is the one Patriarch who we can relate to the most. He struggled for much of his life with numerous painful life circumstances, as many of us can relate to. And yet as much as he was a part of this world, he was also able to cling to God and study His word. The Torah, as the Talmud teaches, is one of the three things which often come through *Yisurim*, that is pains or difficulties. Yet Jacob was able to rise above this, and through his Torah study, was able to become the great Patriarch that he was. Jacob is *our* Patriarch.

The *Lubavitcher Rebbe* also points out that two great personalities died on Shavuot, namely King David and the *Baal Shem Tov*, the founder of Chassidut. The *Rebbe* explains that until the giving of the Torah, the Jewish world was focused on God reaching down to us. When He gave us the Torah it was the ultimate expression of God reaching down to have a connection to us. King David represented through prayer and beginning to build the Temple, the idea of Man reaching up to connect to God. And finally, these two aspects were synthesized in the personality of the Baal Shem Tov. His entire life was spent studying the hidden aspects of Torah, but also reaching out to his fellow man and through unified efforts, reaching up to connect to God through prayer, song and dance. It is this path, the *Rebbe* writes, which will eventually be the path that brings the Messiah, the ultimate Redemption of the world.

Connecting Heaven and Earth

In the Book of Deuteronomy, it is written "Give ear, ye heavens, and I will speak; and let the earth hear the words of my mouth." "Give ear" speaks in the tone of closeness, "let the earth hear" bears the accent of distance. And yet much later in the Torah in the Book of Isaiah it is written "Hear O heavens, and give ear, O earth." Here the relationship implies the opposite, where the Heavens is the one which is distant, and the earth is the one which is close? How are we to reconcile the opposite implications?

I believe there is a very profound lesson contained within this. The Torah as we know means "teaching." Every word is written in a precise way to learn ideas from it. This reverse cannot just be a coincidence. I believe it means that there are times when we feel closest to earth. Perhaps we are doing physical chores, burdened by financial difficulties, or don't feel particularly spiritually motivated. Or perhaps there are times when we feel the opposite. There are times when we feel so connected to God, so inspired that we don't feel the desire to get involved in earthly needs. The Torah teaches that it is here to be the bridge. We are meant to be both simultaneously. The Torah connects us to Heaven in a very real way, but it also doesn't encourage us to be monks living on a mountaintop and removed from the world. God wants us to interact and be a part of this world as well. The Torah creates this incredible dual reality, a slice of Heaven with an appropriate dash of earth as well. Why this dual reality? Because God wanted us to have a relationship with Him. He wanted us to be part of this world, but also at times, with our own free will, be able to rise above it. And the way He gave us to accomplish this is through the Torah.

This idea is hinted to in one of my favorite Midrashic parables. The Midrash is as follows:

> What is the meaning of the verse, "Whatever the Lord wills, he has done in Heaven and on Earth"? This may be compared to a king who decreed, "The Romans may not go to Syria and the Syrians may not go to Rome." Later on, the king desired to marry a Syrian woman, so he abolished the decree, saying, "From now on, Romans may go to Syria and Syrians may go up to Rome, and I shall begin!"
>
> So when the Holy One created His world, He said, "The Heavens are for the Lord and the Earth he has given to the sons of Man." When he desired to give the Torah to His people Israel, He said, "From now on, those above may go up to those below, and those above may go down to those below, and I will go down first!" As it says, "The Lord descended onto Mount Sinai," and afterward, "And onto Moses, He said 'Go up onto the Lord.'" Verily, "Whatever the Lord wills, He has done on Heaven and on Earth!"

And so it is with the giving of the Torah, it serves as the ultimate conduit to the Divine. And once again we see the connection to our Forefather Jacob. It was he who dreamed of the ladder, with angels ascending and descending, connecting Heaven to Earth. It is he, and one he of the Patriarchs who could have this dream, for it is Jacob who represents Torah.

One of my favorite quotes (I am unsure of origin, but I believe it is attributed to Rabbi Chaim Vital, the great disciple of the *Arizal*) is "When we pray, we go up to speak to God. But when we study Torah, God comes down and speaks to us." Torah is the Divine Wisdom He has shared with us. It is filled with stories of inspiration and insight, as well as detailed laws for how to lead a Godly life here on this earth. It is our gift to keep, it is the vehicle to stay inspired, and inspire others. It is the ultimate channel for self-fulfillment here in this world. In short, it is a bridge between heaven and earth.

The Book of Ruth & Shavuot

On the second day of Shavuot, there is a tradition to read the Book of Ruth. Ruth is the story of a Moabite princess named Ruth, who voluntarily chose to follow her mother Naomi to Bethlehem after the passing of her Jewish husband, and well as the passing of her father Elimelech. She moved there even though she would have to endure much hardships, due to her love for Judaism and the God of Israel. Her famous and inspiring words were "Don't urge me to leave you or to turn back from you. Where you go I will go, and where you stay I will stay. Your people will be my people and your God my God." At first, the hardships are nearly unbearable, as she and her mother-in-law are reduced to working in the barley fields just to make ends meet. Eventually, she meets a wealthy kind man named Boaz, in whose eyes she found favor, and he grants her special privileges in the field. Eventually, through a series of remarkable events, Boaz falls in love with Ruth and marries her and provides for her. They have a child named Obed. This child ends up being the grandfather of King David.

On a surface level, there seems to be no connection at all to the Holiday of Shavuot. The events did not take place on Shavuot, and Torah learning is not emphasized at all in the story. What connection does this in any way have to the Holiday celebrating the giving of the Torah?

Several answers are given by the commentators. Some say it is because the Book of Ruth takes place during the harvest season, and Shavuot also takes place during the harvest season. Others also connect Ruth's acceptance of the Jewish faith as analogous to the Jews' acceptance of the

Torah. However, I would like to take this answer and go one step deeper. To me, it is significant where Ruth came from. Although she came from wealth, she came from a background of complete spiritual deprivation. She was a Moabite princess, a culture steeped in pagan worship and immorality. And yet she *voluntarily chose* to leave her wealth and her stature to pursue what she truly believed in; the Jewish faith. She chose to live a life of potential poverty and smallness, an insignificant farm girl who needed to beg for extra grain. And what became of her, after such self-sacrifice? She married a respectable wealthy man and bore a child that became the grandfather of King David! What an inspiring message for Shavuot. This is the incredible power that the Torah has, to bring out extraordinary potential within Man. It is for this reason that I believe Ruth's story is read on Shavuot. For the Torah, especially when it comes with personal self-sacrifice, has the potential to help anyone achieve true greatness, no matter how humble their beginnings may be. It is also, I believe the reason why the giving of the Torah was in *Parshat Yitro* (Torah Portion of Jethro). Yitro also was a high priest of pagan religions, no doubt well respected. He also chose to leave it all to join the Jewish People, as he saw the truth and beauty in the Jewish faith. And what became of him? He ended up becoming in charge of setting up the court system for the entire Jewish People. And his daughter Tzipporah married Moses, the greatest leader the Jewish People have ever had. The Torah is all about potential, no matter what one's beginnings are. Everyone through Torah has the potential for greatness.

A Shavuot Story

The story is told about the *Tzemach Tzedek*, the third Lubavitcher Rebbe, the grandson of the *Rabbi Shneur Zalman of Liadi*, author of the *Tanya*. When the Tzemach Tzedek was only nine or ten years old, he wanted so badly to hear a *shiur* (Torah lecture) from his grandfather, R. Shneur Zalman. The problem was that the *shiur* was only open to the elite Chassidim and took place in R. Shneur Zalman's private study. So, what did the Tzemach Tzedek do? Right outside of the private study was on old furnace that was turned off. The Tzemach Tzedek crawled inside of the furnace and pressed his ear against the wall. When he did this, he was able to hear the entire lecture. This went on for quite some time until one day someone in the house was cold and went to turn on the furnace. Right after turning it on, he right away heard screaming and coughing coming from the inside. Horrified, the person reached inside and pulled out the young boy. Miraculously, the boy had not been hurt yet. By this time, the lecture had stopped and R. Shneur Zalman ran outside to see what was going on. He saw the little boy covered in soot and ashes, coughing and thrashing.

Smiling, R. Shneur Zalman reached down and stroked the little boy's face. "It is a privilege and an honor to have you as a grandchild. Tonight, you have reached a level much higher than anyone who attended my *shiur*. For the Torah was given through fire, the fire of Mount Sinai, and you, who was willing to go through fire to hear words of Torah, will reach heights one day that are unimaginable. What a scholar you will be one day."

This boy, of course, grew up to be the great Tzemach Tzedek, the third Lubavitcher Rebbe, one of the greatest Chassidic leaders in Jewish history.

Although this story did not take place on Shavuot and does not directly involve the Holiday of Shavuot, I believe it is very much a Shavuot story. The story illustrates the internal fire that the truly righteous possess that motivates them to study words of Torah. The question, of course, is: How do we get to that place? How do we get a little taste of what the Tzemach Tzedek already had as a young boy? What can we do, in our own small way, to hear the echo of Mount Sinai? I believe it begins with the paradigm shift discussed in this chapter. Understanding that the Torah is not just an intellectual pursuit, it can bring out the extraordinary potential within Man. And it is the primary vehicle for understanding how to lead a Godly life, how to build character, and develop a relationship with our Creator.

Spiritual Exercises

1. Try to think of a Torah passage that totally inspired you. What aspect of it did you feel you connected with?

2. Try to think of an inspiring figure in Torah who you feel totally speaks to you. What is it about them that you feel you connect with? Try to make it a point to listen to a lecture or class from them as often as you can, even if it is only for a few minutes.

3. Try to set aside a few minutes each day for Torah study, and longer, if the time is available. If possible, learn with a study partner (*Chavruta*) as it can greatly enhance the Torah study in many ways. Monitor how this time changes your life, and how you feel about yourself each day.

4. Try to think of ways to make the Holiday of Shavuot particularly meaningful. Try to imagine as if you are standing that day at the foot of Mount Sinai and witnessing the miracles that occurred. Try to make extra time on Shavuot night itself to learn Torah, as this night is especially powerful for Torah study.

Tisha B'av: Rising from the Ashes

"The joy of my heart ceased when my enemies caused me to hear: "Depart from me, the Land of Israel!" They degraded me and made me feel like refuse among the peoples of the world. You placed a barrier above Your Dwelling-place so as not to hear my prayers. You have separated Yourself. My heroes were humbled; my enemies clapped their hands and caused my limbs to tremble. They destroyed my mighty men."

-A Dirge from the Tisha B'av Liturgy

I F ONE WAS TO LABEL the Jewish Story with one word, more than likely the word which would be chosen would be "tragedy." Perhaps no other people on earth has known tragedy quite like the Jewish People; from Biblical times till the present day. Sadly enough, many Jews have left the fold due to overwhelming feeling of loss, of forever feeling like the victim instead of the victor. This feeling culminated over 65 years ago, when our People experienced a loss like none other in our blood-soaked history. It is a loss that our People have never fully recovered from, and perhaps never will.

Delving into Tisha B'av means delving into the darkest places of the Jewish story. This chapter will not only discuss the many tragedies which have befallen our People, but some of their deeper significances, and perhaps even glean a perspective which can be beneficial for our own spiritual growth.

All is Contained in the Beginning

In Jewish tradition, we are taught that all can be learned from the beginning of a concept; that is, when it is first mentioned in the Torah. We find the first mention of Tisha B'av not explicitly in the text, but in *Rashi,* the great medieval commentator.

This refence is in the Torah. Many of us are aware of the Sin of the Spies when they went out to scout the Land of Israel. Instead of being able to see the extraordinary beauty and majesty of the Land of Israel, they came back with a very negative report, saying that the Land would be too hard to conquer. The verse tells us that "they wept that night." Rashi explains that this night was Tisha B'av. Since they had wept for no purpose, as their faith in God was weak, God said he would give them a reason to weep on that night throughout history. Indeed, it became true. Not only were both Holy Temples destroyed on that day, but even throughout history up until the present day many tragedies have occurred on Tisha B'av. Both the 1st Crusade as well as the English and Spanish Inquisition occurred on Tisha B'av. And World War I, which World War II was a continuation of, began on Tisha B'av. The deportation of Jews from Warsaw, the largest Jewish Ghetto, began on Tisha B'av. And Auschwitz, the largest concentration camp was opened on Tisha B'av. The list continues.

Somehow, the Sin of the Spies contained the ultimate tragedy that is Tisha B'av. How are we to understand this? Perhaps the key component is that it wasn't just the Spies that sinned, it was the entire Jewish People for believing the report. It is important to remember that these were the very same Jews who had just witnessed extraordinary miracles; namely the Splitting of the Sea and the Ten Plagues. And yet these very same people could not muster up the simple faith in God that He would deliver them as He had done before. God, we are taught, mimics our actions, as we are taught in Psalms "God is our Shadow." When we push Him away, He pushes us away, or to put it more accurately, He *allows us to push Him away.* This means He does not intervene on behalf of His People, but allows Nature to take its course, so to speak. And thus, tragedies occur. This was written in perhaps the most well-known verse in the list of curses in the Torah "And I shall surely Hide My Face from you." And so, this incident created a blemish in the Jewish People, one which we still feel reverberations from until this very day.

This of course does not mean that the Sin of the Spies is the sole reason for all of our suffering, or even that we know much of the reasons for any of our suffering. I have always believed that anyone who claims to know the reason for our suffering, including the Holocaust, is either extremely arrogant or disillusioned. The Sin of the Spies just created a possible *opening* for such tragedies to occur in the first place.

The God of Suffering, the God of Joy

In the Book of Zechariah, we are taught that in Messianic times "On that Day, God will be One and His Name will be One." The Talmud asks what is this supposed to mean? Isn't God One right now? Why only in the Messianic times? The Talmud gives a very astute answer: In future times, we will see that really *all* is somehow for our good, that the God of our suffering is somehow the same God of our joy. In the end, it will be revealed that even our suffering was somehow for our ultimate good.

In a similar vein, the Talmud teaches that on hearing good news we say the blessing "Blessed is the Good, and the One who creates Good." Upon hearing bad news, one says "Blessed is the true Judge." However, the Talmud then says a seemingly impossible task; we must make the blessing on the bad news with the same joyous fervor that one makes on the blessing for good! How are to understand this? Indeed, it takes a tremendous amount of faith to attain this level, but it is the ultimate acceptance of the Goodness of God. It is for this reason, perhaps, that the Talmud goes on to say that in the Messianic era, there will be only one blessing, and that is the blessing we say on good news. For in the future, when we attain a higher awareness, we will be able to see clearly how even negative news is for our ultimate good.

Perhaps this is the reason why the Talmud says that one who accepts bad news with joy brings salvation to the world. For when one accepts difficult news with the joy that this is somehow for a greater good, it brings the world one step closer to the final redemption when we will indeed see that it all was for our ultimate good.

These ideas are even hinted at within Tisha B'av itself. On Tisha

B'av we don't say *Tachanun* in our morning prayers, a sad supplication which is usually omitted on holidays and joyous occasions. Why, of all days, would it be omitted on Tisha B'av? The answer is that on a deep level, Tisha B'av *is*, in fact, a joyous occasion, as not only is there hope within our suffering that one day our suffering will end, but there will be a day when we will understand how our suffering was for our own greater good.

This idea can be seen even within the words of *Eicha* (Lamentations). *Eicha* is read on Tisha B'av and it was written by the Prophet Jeremiah as he bemoans the destruction of Jerusalem and the Holy Temple which he foresaw. It is, without a doubt, the saddest book of the Biblical canon. And yet it is written "Awaken and rejoice at night." *Eliyahu Hanavi* (Elijah the Prophet) expounds that the verse uses the word *Rina*, to describe rejoicing. Rina is used when describing rejoicing during suffering. This is alluded to with the word "night" in the verse which is usually an allegory to difficult times.

Furthermore, King David whose life was replete with personal misfortune and suffering wrote in Psalms "at midnight I will rise to praise you on your righteous judgments." This was also a reference to stern judgments and suffering as King David could see how even his suffering was for his own ultimate good.

Once again, I would like to reiterate that this is an extremely lofty level of faith that has been attained by very few people. I most certainly have not attained this level. But at the end of the day, what choice do we have but to accept that it is somehow for our ultimate good? There are only two other options to explain our suffering, and both are equally as miserable as the other. One would be that there really is no God, everything is just random. But this would mean our suffering indeed serves no greater purpose, it is all just random, and there is no reward and punishment after the grave. The other explanation is that God is not really a Loving God at all, and he enjoys inflicting harm on his creations. Can anyone really say that they want to accept these other two alternatives?

Tisha B'av teaches us that it is okay to cry. It is okay to grieve. We are all human. This is part of the human condition to feel pain, both emotional and physical. But Tisha B'av also teaches us that we can take comfort that there is a greater purpose out there, and one day we will receive true comfort, and one day we will understand.

Looking Differently at God's Role

In *Shir Hashirim* (Song of Songs) it is written "God gazes at us through the windows and peeks at us through the cracks." What does this mean? I once heard a beautiful parable from *Rabbi Moshe Weinberger* in the name of the great Chassidic Master, the *Bnei Yissoschor*. He says it is like a mother who is watching over her child through an open window. She does this during times when her child is loving and obedient. However, there are times when the child's behavior has angered his mother. During these times it appears that the mother doesn't want to see this child, and the blinds on the window remain closed. During this time, the child may naturally feel abandoned. However, unbeknownst to the child, his mother is still peeking "through the cracks," so to speak, at her child. Her love for him never dies. No matter where the child is, he is not abandoned.

I want to share with you one of the most beautiful quotes I have ever read. It is from the great *Rabbi Joseph B. Soloveitchik*, regarded by many as the preeminent Jewish Philosopher and scholar of the 20th century. This is what he wrote, when he was going through the loss of a loved one:

"As a rule, in times of joy and elation, one finds God's footsteps in the majesty and grandeur of the cosmos, in its vastness and its stupendous dynamics. When man is drunk with life, when he feels that living is a dignified affair, then man beholds God in infinity. In moments of ecstasy God addresses Himself to man through the twinkling stars and the roar of the endlessly distant heavens: "O Lord my God Thou are very great, Thou are clothed with glory and majesty." In such moments, Majestas Dei, which not even the vast universe is large enough to accommodate, addresses itself to happy man. However, with the arrival of the dark night of the soul, in moments of agony and black despair, when living becomes ugly and absurd; plainly nauseating, when man loses his sense of beauty and majesty, God addresses him, not from infinity but from the infinitesimal, not from the vast stretches of the universe but from a single spot in the darkness which surrounds suffering man, from within the black despair itself... God, in those moments, appeared not as the exalted, majestic King, but rather as a humble, close friend, brother, father: in such moments of black despair, He was not far from me; He was right there in the dark room; I felt His warm Hand, so to speak, on my shoulder, I hugged His Knees. He was with me in the narrow confines of a small room, taking up no space at all. God's abiding in a fenced-in finite locus manifests His humility and love for man. In such moments Humilitas Dei, which resides in the humblest and tiniest of places, addresses itself to man."

I love this quote because I believe it touches upon a very different notion of God. God plays different roles in our lives, and therefore can be seen differently, and in fact, *is meant* to be seen differently, depending on our life circumstances. There are times God is meant to be experienced as the Omnipotent One, who has created and sustains all that we see. But there are times, those Tisha B'av times, when God is simply our friend, one who wants nothing more than to hold us and comfort us. This is the feeling we can all have on Tisha B'av. *"Emo anochi Batzarah,"* God is with us in suffering, as the Torah writes. It is still an opportunity to get close to Him, but in a different way than we feel at happier times. But He is very much there in those moments as well.

A Tisha B'av Story

The following is a legendary story involving Emperor Napoleon Bonaparte. He was once travelling with his soldiers through a small Jewish village in Europe and came across a Jewish synagogue. Inside, Jews were weeping while they prayed and were sitting on the floor. Curious about what was going on, he asked one of his guards who was more familiar with Jewish tradition. The guard responded that it was Tisha B'av, a day commemorating the destruction of both the 1st and

2nd Holy Temples. Since then, the guard continued, the Jews have been scattered all over the world and have endured much persecution. On this day, the Jews fast and pray and read the Book of Lamentations, which was written as a sad eulogy for the destruction of the Temple and its subsequent exile.

Napoleon inquired when were the Temples destroyed. He was astounded when he heard that the most recent Temple was destroyed nearly 2,000 years ago. When he heard this, he exclaimed "A people who can mourn so emotionally over a Temple that fell 2,000 years ago, will surely live to see it rebuilt!"

This is of course the secret to Jewish survival. It is our tenacity despite all odds. It is the collective memory of the Jewish People, that we continue to keep alive. That both our tragedies and our triumphs are of equal importance to us. We continue to relive each with the same passion and fervor as if they had just occurred. And Napoleon was absolutely right. We will live to see it rebuilt and our honor once again restored. Let that great day come very soon. Amen.

Spiritual Exercises

1. Take a little bit of time to learn more about the sad events that are commemorated on Tisha B'av. This should include recent tragedies as well. As difficult as it may be, try to envision as if you were there when these tragedies occurred.

2. Try to take some time to study *Eicha* (the Book of Lamentations). There are many wonderful commentaries on it to help enhance it's meaning and bring the words to life. There are audio classes on it available online as well.

3. Learn more about the greatest tragedy in modern Jewish history, the Holocaust. Although it is not an event exclusively related to Tisha B'av, it is epic in scope, and a tragedy which is more relatable to us.

4. Try to think about tragedies that have occurred in your own life. How did you react to them? How did you feel toward God during those times? Are there lessons that you have learned from those experiences? Did they enhance or detract from your relationship with God? Are there ways you can think of that you can use those experiences to enhance your relationship with God?

Tu B'Av: The Jewish Holiday of Love

"May it be Your will, Hashem, our Father, King of the Universe, that I find my true marriage partner without difficulties of any kind. Guide and lead us to each other and open our eyes and hearts to make the right decision."

-Prayer for Finding a Soulmate

IT HAS BEEN CALLED THE Jewish Holiday of Love, or as some affectionately call it, the Jewish Valentine's Day. Throughout Israel, it has become a popular day for Jewish weddings. And both in Israel and throughout the Diaspora, it has become a popular day for singles events, to try to meet one's soulmate.

Tu B'av is not a well-known holiday and is considered by most to be a minor holiday as there are no commanded rituals in honor of the day. There are no special prayers associated with the day in the *Siddur* (prayer book). However, it still earns a very rightful place in the Jewish Calendar. For Judaism is all about love. And not only the love between us and God, but also the love between Man and Wife.

Indeed, right at the beginning of the Torah, we are taught with the creation of Adam "And God spoke 'It is not good for Man to be alone. I will make for him a helpmate opposite him.'" Indeed, the Torah is replete with stories which emphasize the love between a man and a woman. Perhaps the most well-known is the story of Jacob and Rachel. Jacob worked seven years for Laban to be with his love Rachel, and then worked yet another seven years after Laban deceived him. And yet incredibly the Torah writes that although it was fourteen years before he

152

was finally able to marry her, that time seemed to go by quickly. How are we to understand this? One would think that all of that time would have seemed forever as it was time away from his beloved? However, Jacob knew the secret of true love. Love is much more about giving than receiving. He thought of those 14 years as giving wholeheartedly to his beloved, and therefore it wasn't detracting from his love, it was only building it. Therefore, the time seemed to go by quickly since he saw that time as an opportunity to increase his love for her. It is well known that even the Hebrew word *Ahavah* comes from the root word Hav, which means to Give. For through giving, one comes to grow into love. This is a beautiful and healthy way to look at love. Every obstacle can be an opportunity to grow even deeper in love, as it becomes an opportunity to give to the significant other.

So now back to Tu B'av itself. The Bible makes no explicit mention of this mysterious holiday. So where did Tu B'av originate from? And how has it evolved into what it is today?

Early Origins

Although not explicitly mentioned in the Torah, Tu B'av had its origins in the Five Book of Moses with the *Daughters of Tzelafchad*. Originally, orphaned women who had no brothers were only allowed to marry within their own tribe to prevent their fathers' land in Israel from being passed on to other tribes. However, after much arbitration, it was decided that these women could in fact, marry men from other tribes. According to the commentaries, this decision occurred on Tu B'av in the 40th year of the Jewish encampment in the Wilderness. That same year, the last of the generation of the Sin of the Spies, which had been forbidden to enter the Promised Land, found that they were not destined to die. For forty years, every Tisha B'av night, the Jews made graves for themselves in which they slept on Tisha B'Av; every year a proportion of them died. In the 40th year, the fifteen thousand who had remained from the first generation went to sleep in the graves and woke up the next day to their surprise. Thinking they made a mistake with the date, they kept sleeping in the graves they had dug until they reached Tu B'Av and saw a full moon. Only then did they know that the decree had ended and they were allowed to live.

Tu B'av continued to have significance in both the Prophets and the Writings portion of the written Torah. It is when the Tribe of Benjamin was able to marry outside of its own tribe in the Book of Judges after it was punished for a disgraceful incident involving a concubine. It was the day when King Hosea of the Northern Kingdom removed the sentries that were blocking the roads to Jerusalem, once again allowing the Ten Tribes to gain access to the Temple. After the failed Bar Kochba rebellion, the Roman occupiers allowed burial of the Jews who were slaughtered in battle. The day they allowed it was Tu B'av. Miraculously, the bodies that had been left on the battlefield for an entire year had not decomposed. It was also the day when the cutting of the wood for the year in the Temple service was completed. And finally, Tu B'av was the beginning of the grape harvest season.

It was this last one, which led to great celebrations which is what Tu B'av became most known for. The Talmud says in celebration of the grape harvest, young unmarried maidens used to come out dressed in white, dancing in the vineyards, and in search of a potential mate. Thus, began the Tu B'av tradition of searching for a soulmate, of searching for love. This must have been the first Jewish Singles events! (My how we have evolved ever since!) This tradition of searching for love has continued to this day and has expanded to include celebrating love as well.

Judaism: The Religion of Love

Unfortunately, many people have a preconceived notion that Judaism is all about fire and brimstone and has very little if anything to do with God's love for us. In fact, nothing could be further from the truth. The Torah in fact, never calls Judaism a religion at all. The only time Judaism was called "Religion" in the Torah was said by our enemy Haman, and he was sorely mistaken. Judaism is all about *relationship,* that is, establishing and deepening our relationship with our Creator. Perhaps the word most associated with God is "Echad" which means Oneness. It is no coincidence that the *Gematria* (numerical value) of this word is 13, the same number as the word *Ahavah,* which means Love. It is also the number of the Attributes of Divine Mercy that the Torah lists. It is also the age when a boy becomes obligated to observe the Mitzvot, and his relationship with His creator really begins.

But perhaps the most significant place where we see Judaism as a way to develop a relationship with our Creator is in *Shir Hashirim*, The Song of Songs. According to most of the major commentators, including *Rashi*, this entire book, which appears to be a simple love poem, is an allegory for the love between God and the Jewish People. Here in the allegory, we see all of the emotional highs and lows that often accompany a physical relationship between Man and Woman. We experience the intense feeling of yearning for the other, the feeling of closeness with intimacy, the times of faithfulness and faithlessness, of fidelity and infidelity. It talks of the times of distance and separation, but ultimately, love prevails, and a great reunion takes place, as it will one day between God and His People in Messianic times.

As such, I believe Tu B'av is not only a time to rekindle our love for our spouse or to strengthen our search for our spouse. It is also a time to strengthen the bond with our Creator, with whom we also share a deep love, and our relationship in many ways, mirrors the relationships we have here during our lifetime.

A Modern Day Tu B'Av Story

I remember hearing this story many years ago at an inspirational *Shabbaton* (weekend retreat) and it has stayed with me ever since. The story took place on Tu B'av itself. Every day, Jewish singles of all walks of life travel to a deep valley just on the outskirts of Safed named Amuka. Therein lies the grave of the great Talmudic Sage Rabbi Yonatan Ben Uziel, and they come to pray for a *Shidduch* (match). Rabbi Yonatan Ben Uziel, the greatest pupil of Rabbi Hillel, himself only married much later in life and was therefore unable to fulfill the commandment to be fruitful and multiply. Legend has it that on his deathbed, he told his disciples that anyone who wished to get married should pray at his gravesite and he would beseech the Almighty fervently on their behalf.

The story is about a young Yeshiva student whose family had made *Aliyah* (moved to Israel) from the US. He had recently completed his training in the IDF and wished to return to learn Torah for a few years before beginning university. Feeling bad for a few older friends of his who were still single, he decided to pray for them at the grave of Rabbi Yonatan in the valley of Amuka. And what better day to pray for them than on Tu B'av itself! At the gravesite itself there was separate seating for men and women, but when he came out after praying, he nearly collided with a young woman coming out. Startled, a little paper that she kept folded in her *Siddur* (prayer book) fell out.

"Hey, you dropped this," he said, and reached down to pick it up for her. "Thank you," she replied, as she looked at him and smiled. For the first time, he got a glimpse of her face. She radiated with a warmth and beauty that he rarely had ever seen. "Is this a list of people you prayed for?" He asked innocently. "Yes," she replied. "They are some older single women I know from my community who have been looking for a match for a long time." He smiled broadly in return. "I also came here to pray with a list of some older friends of mine. I notice you speak English well, without any accent. Were you born in the States?" "Yes," she replied. "My family made Aliyah about 5 years ago."

And so the conversation began. Two Americans whose families had made Aliyah around the same time. Both had done their national service. Both were into Judaism and spiritual growth, but with a little more of a modern outlook. Both had a strong passionate Zionistic souls. And perhaps, most importantly, both had come to pray at Rabbi Yonatan's grave on Tu B'av, not for themselves, but for others. And according to Jewish tradition, when one prays sincerely for others, his or her own prayers are often answered. And so their courtship began. One year later, on Tu B'av again, they got married. And every year, on their Tu B'av anniversary, they would celebrate near Rabbi Yonatan's grave, and once again, pray for singles who needed their prayers.

So, whoever said there is no love or romance in Judaism? Everything in its time and place. My blessing to all singles is to be able to find quickly and smoothly the significant other who will bring more completeness and fulfillment to their lives. And for those who have already found that special someone to feel and appreciate that love for each other, and every day it should only expand and grow.

Spiritual Exercises

1. Try to remember a time when you experienced true love. If you have never experienced this, perhaps try to identify what may be holding you back from experiencing love.

2. Try to take a few minutes to study the Jewish views on Love. Perhaps study some of the more romantic love stories in the Torah. How are they similar to the Western world? How are they different?

3. If you have a significant other in your life, try to appreciate them for a few minutes each day. Try to remember their qualities that made you fall in love in the beginning. In this way, your feelings of love will always be renewed.

Afterword

The Cycle of Jewish Living

"If you study the rhythm of life on this planet, you will find that everything moves in perfect symphony with everything else — by grand Divine design. The earth has the ability to heal and regenerate itself, just as our oceans have the ability to replenish themselves by turning over their debris with the waves to wash them ashore. This perfect orchestration of the cycle of life is one of the Creator's greatest and most beautiful miracles... Such is also the story of the sun and moon, of me and you. Nothing truly dies. All energy simply transforms."

-Suzy Kassem

ALL OF LIFE IS CYCLIC. This is true in virtually every sphere of life, whether cosmic, earth, animal, plant, or human. The earth revolves annually around the sun, the moon orbits the earth monthly, as we all know. Plant and animal life grow through their lifelong cycle, die, and then others are reborn in their place. And of course, in human life, we are born, live our time here on this earth, and then pass away, to be reborn again, in the Jewish tradition, in a different form in the Next World. And most of those that are born will one day become parents themselves, giving the Gift of Life that they received to someone else. And for each death that occurs in this world, someone somewhere is being born. And so, the cycle continues.

Cycles occur in the yearly seasons as well. The seasons begin with

159

spring, the flowers bloom, the trees blossom. It continues through the summer, when it reaches its peak. And then autumn comes, and the leaves begin to fall. Soon it is winter, and all has seemingly withered and died. But just when it seems as if all hope is lost, spring once again overtakes the seasons, the petals begin to bloom, and the earth begins anew.

The Jewish Cycle of course is no different. Each year we go through the same cycles in both our personal lives and in our Jewish lives. There are times in our lives when we feel distant from God, only to once again feel the return that we experience on Rosh Hashanah and Yom Kippur. We experience the difficulties and coldness of winter, and the winter Holidays are signified with this, namely Purim and Chanukah. Both stories appear to have occurred naturally, with God's involvement. Only those who witnessed the miracle of Chanukah in the Temple knew the true nature of the events taking place. And in Purim, one needs to study the story on a deeper level to see God's involvement. The beginning of the Hebrew calendar year begins with Passover. Passover and Shavuot occur during the spring, the time of rebirth and renewal, the time we were forged into a People. And so, also in Jewish terms, the cycle continues.

On a National level, we have experienced cycles as well. There were times in our history, like on Tisha B'av and during the Holocaust when the Jewish People experienced loss and sadness. On Passover we experienced true freedom, on Chanukah and Purim we experienced salvation, and on Yom Hatzmaut we experienced a return to our Homeland. All of life cycles, on a personal level, on a yearly level, and on a National level are all connected.

But I want to again mention the same words I began this book with, for I believe now these words will have a more profound meaning. *The Jewish calendar is not a circle, but rather a spiral.* This means that we do not arrive at the same place we were at last year when we reach a holiday, but we have all hopefully grown to a higher place. This is means not only have we reached a higher spiritual place, but we also have a greater understanding and appreciation for the holiday you have reached. This takes hard work, but true growth, as we all know, comes when you step out of your comfort zone. For some people, this may mean a greater diligence to adherence of the Jewish rituals and customs associated with each holiday. For others, it may be diving into a deeper understanding of each holiday. For most, it will be a combination of both. For through understanding the holidays better, we naturally want to take on a greater adherence to the *Mitzvot* associated with each holiday. Each Holiday is an opportunity for retrospection. Where was I, spiritually speaking, last year during the Holiday? Have I taken the opportunity to grow in my appreciation for it? Have I uncovered new facets of the Holiday that I have not seen before?

The great *Rebbe Nachman of Breslov* once wrote about *Simanim Baderech,* that is, Road Marks along the path. In this Journey called Life, it is often so easy to get lost. The Holidays are the Road Marks, they are the periodical guides along the way to help give us direction. But there is always more to learn from each of these great days. I know for myself, although writing this book has certainly enhanced my appreciation for the Holidays and has helped my own growth, I still have much more to learn and gain. The Jewish Journey always continues.

I wanted to end the book with a blessing. According to Jewish tradition, we are taught never to take any blessing lightly for every blessing has some significance, whether we see it or not. I want to bless everyone to have a greater appreciation and understanding of each Holiday. I want to bless everyone to be able to fulfill each Holiday to the best of his or her ability. And I bless everyone to use the Holidays to enhance their own Judaism and in turn, become happier more fulfilled people.

With Love,

Yisroel

Biographies

Aaron, Rabbi David. Founder of Isralight (1986) and author of the best-selling Endless Light, Seeing God, and Love is My Religion.

Baal Shem Tov. Rabbi Israel ben Eliezer, eighteenth- century founder of Chassidut. He experienced a spiritual enlightenment while secluded in the Carpathian Mountains, and taught a doctrine of ecstatic mysticism.

Bnai Yissoschor, The. Rabbi Eliezer Spira, the founder of Munkach Chassidim, he was a close disciple of the Chozer of Lublin (Seer of Lublin), and authored many works, most notably the Bnai Yissaschar, a series of mystical interpretations of the Torah.

Elimelech of Lizensk, Rebbe. A close disciple of the Maggid of Mezerich, one of the early founders of the Chassidic movement, he authored the famous Noam Elimelech and is the subject of numerous legendary stories with his brother Reb Zusha.

Hutner, Rabbi Yitzchak. Leader of the famed Yeshiva in New York Yeshivas Chaim Berlin, he authored several works including the famous Pachad Yitzchak, a series of mystical interpretations of the Torah.

Jungreis, Rebbetzin Esther: Founder of Hineni organization, and a Holocaust survivor, she has authored The Committed Life along with many other titles

Klausenberger Rebbe. (Rabbi Yekusiel Yakov Halberstam) The founder of the Sanz-Klausenberg Chassidic dynasty, he was a Holocaust survivor who lost his family during the war, but later remarried, moved to Israel and founded a voluntary non profit hospital.

Kook, Rabbi Abraham Isaac. The first chief rabbi of then- Palestine, now Israel, he wrote extensively on Jewish mysticism, aesthetics, and one of the early proponents of a religious Zionist movement.

Kotzker Rebbe. A nineteenth-century Chassidic rabbi who devoted his life to teaching about personal analysis and introspection. He burned all of his writings before his death, but his teachings and stories live on in an oral tradition.

Levi Yitzchak of Berditchev, Rabbi. One of the main students of the Maggid of Mezeritch, he was famous for interpreting people's actions positively, and also wrote Kedushat Levi, a multi-volume commentary on the Torah.

Lubavitcher Rebbe, The. (Rabbi Menachem Mendel Schneerson) The most influential rabbi in modern history, he mobilized a movement with thousands of Chabad centers throughout the world. To date, there are over 200 volumes of his lectures on a large variety of Jewish topics.

Moshe Leib Sossover, Rabbi. A third-generation Chassidic spent much time redeeming Jews from captivity, since it was common for the authorities to kidnap Jews for ransom.

Nachman of Breslov, Rebbe. The great-grandson of the Baal Shem Tov, he revived Chassidic tradition through combining Torah scholarship together with deep esoteric Torah wisdom, as well as stories and parables.

Nachmanides (Ramban). A great Medieval scholar and philosopher, he wrote a commentary to the Five Books of Moses. He was also well known for successfully defending Judaism against the apostate Pablo Christiani in the presence of King James of Aragon.

Rashi. Rabbi Solomon ben Isaac, an eleventh-century French rabbi and teacher, prolific scholar and commentator on the Hebrew Bible,

Talmud, his works are of primary significance for proper understanding of traditional Jewish teachings

Shafier Rabbi Binyamin. Founder of the popular website theshmuz. com, he offers insightful advice on daily concerns shared by all and has developed these talks into a series of books.

Shneur Zalman of Liadi, Rabbi. The founder of Chabad Chassidut, and student of the Maggid of Mezeritch, he authored a commentary on Shulchan Aruch, but is well known for the Tanya, a blend of the mystical and intellectual teachings that Chabad Chassidim study daily.

Soloveichik, Rabbi Ahron. The brother of the famed Rabbi J.B. Soloveitchik, he taught at Yeshivah University for many decades and authored many works, including Logic of the Heart, Logic of the Mind.

Soloveitchik, Rabbi Joseph B. A twentieth-century rabbi who received rabbinic ordination in Europe and a Ph.D. in Jewish philosophy, he moved to America in the 1930's, and he revitalized Yeshiva University in New York City, where many of his students became prominent rabbis, developing a Jewish philosophy that merged rationalism and mysticism.

Spira, Rabbi Yisroel. A member of the Bluzhiver dynasty, he was a Holocaust survivor, but his wife and children were murdered during the war, and he later moved to Brooklyn and then Israel.

Tatz. Rabbi Akiva: A former doctor who later became an observant rabbi, he is today a highly sought after speaker on many mystical subjects, and is a prolific author

Tzadok of Lublin, Rabbi. An eighteenth-century rabbi and author who devoted the first part of his life to studying "revealed texts" like the Talmud, and then devoted the rest of his life to studying and commenting on the esoteric Jewish writings.

Tzemach Tzedek. (Rabbi Menachem Mendel Schneerson) The third Rebbe of the Chabad dynasty, he was known as the *Tzemach*

Tzedek ("Righteous Sprout" or "Righteous Scion"), after the title of a voluminous compendium of *Halacha* (Jewish law) that he authored. He also authored *Derech Mitzvotecha* ("Way of Your Commandments"), a mystical exposition of the *Mitzvos*.

Weinberger, Rabbi Moshe. The Rabbi of Congregation Aish Kodesh in Woodmere and Spiritual Mentor at Yeshiva University, Rabbi Weinberger is a prominent lecturer in the Chassidic community.

www.ingramcontent.com/pod-product-compliance
Lightning Source LLC
Chambersburg PA
CBHW031847090426
42741CB00005B/388